Asanga Angya

FREEDOM BEYOND MIND & TIME

EASTERN PHILOSOPHY – WESTERN PSYCHOLOGY

ISBN 978-953-48429-0-4

(paperback)

ISBN 978-953-48429-1-1

(EPUB)

ISBN 978-953-48429-2-8

(Kindle MOBI)

Self published in 2019 by

Asanga Angya

FREEDOM BEYOND MIND & TIME

Eastern Philosophy – Western Psychology

Essays about Path of Self-Knowledge

by Asanga Angya

Self-enquiry leads directly to Self-realization by removing the obstacles which make you think that the Self is not already realized.

Ramana Maharshi

In order to break out of a prison, one first must confess to being in a prison. The trap is man's emotional structure, his character structure. There is little use in devising systems of thought about the nature of the trap if the only thing to do in order to get out of the trap is to know the trap and to find the exit.

Wilhelm Reich

CONTENT

TEN LINKS IN TAMING THE IMAGINARY

A short summary of this handbook in several points

Understanding this is just the beginning or the Philosophy of Self-knowledge; applying this is the development or Art of Self--knowledge. Living from step to step, from breath to breath is the actualization or Wisdom of Self-knowledge; moreover, this unutterable Path.

I. When infinite omnipresent consciousness (*chit*) manifests this universe it releases all its energy which had hitherto been dormant in potency. The released energy (*mahashakti*) is the same as the Universal Mind (*chitishakti*) which takes on all of manifest creation's forms. This creative and projective activity (*vikshepa*) of the Universal Mind creates a veil that hides (*avarana*) the *Universe's True Nature* or *Brahman.*

II. At the same time this, primary, unlimited Mind creating, reflecting and identifying itself with all manifested phenomena becomes limited, individualized and conditioned by the attributes of a particular phenomenon. Thus, when human being's *conditioned mind* identifies with a physical form, it automatically projects the illusory, personal ego (*ahamkara*) as its own image. The conditioned mind's *imaginative activity* also creates a veil that hides the true nature of human beings, or the *Self* (*atman*).

III.   The ego then does everything to preserve the *self-image* which it presents to the world and with which it hides its falsity, illusiveness, and absurdness. This image is the ego's mask, or in terms of depth psychology, its *persona*.

IV.   The ego represses all of the mind's contents which do not agree with the persona into the mind's subconscious state. Also, much of the mind's karmically accumulated contents which that ego has not yet awakened steer it from the unconscious part of the mind. This part along with the subconscious comprises, in depth psychology terms, man's *psychic Shadow (chitta)*.

V.   Thus, the functionally *divided mind* is a permanent source of internal conflict and suffering for its separator, the ego. Namely, the ego wants the yearned-for serenity and bliss, but in such a manner that it can continue to rule with its "divide and rule" strategy. It is crucified on the cross that it has built for itself, and out of delusion and bitterness it crucifies its neighbors along with itself, not knowing how to get down from that cross.

VI.   There is no way out for the ego, because the ego itself is a lie and a phantom. But there is an exit or *passage to freedom* for the Consciousness that in purified mind, like in a mirror, sees its True Nature. The following proverb depicts the true relationship between the True Nature and the ego: "*A diamond, even when it falls into the mud, remains a diamond. Dust, even when it soars up to the heavens, remains dust*". But the diamond needs to be taken out of the mud and carefully cleaned if we want it to see our True Nature reflected in it like in a mirror.

VII.   For this only Mind is a mirror in a twofold sense:

    x) in the Universal Mind, the all-creating Consciousness reflects all its hitherto unexpressed potential and through this self-mirroring manifests creation;

    y) in the individual mind that same Consciousness reflects its own forgotten but never lost True Nature; and returns to its Self through that self-reflection, beyond all manifestations and projections.

VIII. In both cases, the "trigger," whether for *manifestation* or *self-reflection*, is the question that wakes in the essence of *Consciousness* itself, and that is the fundamental question of its self-determination or self-identification, "*Who am I?*" (*Koham?*).

IX.   Should there be *manifestation*, the answer to this question is the release and affirmation of Absolute Consciousness's energy *(chitishakti)*, in the form of this creation.

X.   Should there be *self-reflection* the answer to the same is question is the mind's liberation from identification with phenomena from the manifested world, withdrawal and turning consciousness's energy away from creation and towards its own Source and the actualization of Original Nature, which at the moment of awakening presents itself as *Self-illuminating Consciousness.*

P. S. Just like Kakuan attempted to concisely and practically exhibit complex Buddhist teachings about understanding and disciplining the mind in his "Ten Ox Herding Pictures," the aim of these ten steps is to try to sum up the *ten links* that *universal Consciousness's* closed, unbreakable *chain of manifesta-*

tion and self-reflection is comprised of; a chain that seemingly enslaves and seemingly frees.

That is why they are called "Ten links in taming the Imaginary", because the whole process of manifestation and identification as well as self-reflection and emancipation of that one and the same undivided and unconditional Consciousness is a pure creative figment of the imagination, while only *self-Consciousness* (or the Absolute's Self-consciousness) that is at the basis of all imaginary phenomena, states and processes is *real, lasting and unconditional.*

But understanding this is just the beginning or the *Philosophy of Self-knowledge*; applying this is the development or *Art of Self-knowledge.* Living from step to step, from breath to breath is the actualization or *Wisdom of Self-knowledge*; moreover, this unutterable Path.

Nothing more can be said of this, all that is left is to travel...

On the lonely path,

empty,

inexhaustible...

PROLOGUE

Though he carries the Wise man on his shoulders,
the fool will ask the blind man for the Way

That is why true Wisdom and true Art, just like Tao and Te, can only be that which we create from our inner Being. The external products of this process (in the form of books or other works) are but the sandy tiles of the path on which we pass, fragmented traces along the way, which will one day be shaken off our Self like dust off an outworn shoe.

Perhaps the views expressed here may come across as the fruits of the cynical perception of the world and of life. The matter at hand here is not cynicism, rather the immediate realization that the affirmation of life can only be experienced in its entirety from the very *core* of one's being. But this is not possible until the *core* is freed from the many layers of the egocentric cover woven by illusion.

The aim of this book therefore is to point out all the many and varied illusions that we feed with our unconscious habits, prejudices and identifications. Once illusions are identified and released, anyone can find their own way *home*.

In this respect, these short and compressed reflections do not require any special schooling; they do, however, require focused attention and are worded in such a way as to open up the problem that is to be considered, to illuminate the shadowed oversights or accentuate the uncritically accepted prejudices which are ready for a deep review.

For the honest seeker will never be satisfied with pre-prepared answers, garnished and served on a kitschy platter, as he knows that the answer that can transform him must come from within. As the classic Taoist Chuang Tzu would say, teachings and praxis are the net with which we catch fish (that is, experience), and once the fish is caught the net can be forgotten. But from personal experience I would add that all fish may not be caught with the same net, and that all fish do not take the same bait.

That is why *true Wisdom* and *true Art*, just like *Tao and Te*, can only be that which we create from our inner Being. The external products of this process (in the form of books or other works) are but the sandy tiles of the path on which we pass, fragmented traces along the way, which will one day be shaken off our *Self* like dust off an outworn shoe.

It is important to understand that these insights' approach is guided by the principle of *negative path*, as its goal is to bring to consciousness and empower that which we *are not* in order to awaken that which we *are*. There are two types of travelers, followers and explorers. For the former, the path he identifies with is the *positive path*, all he needs is faith. For the latter, the path that must be re-examined is the *negative path*; research and personal experience is what matters.

Only those who are afraid of life and who want to control it at all costs shackle their lives to principles and rules, whether they be religious, moralistic or ideological. By overlooking the direct experience of *reality* beyond principles and rules, they deny themselves the opportunity to experience personal insight, which life is really about.

There is no perfect system. If the mind were able to build a perfect system, like light through a black hole, consciousness would not be able to break through the virtual trap, and man would not be able to see through the mind's illusion; he could not wake up from the *place where his dreams are woven*.

Fortunately, every mind created system has its gap, primarily because the mind is the biggest gap in the system. The man who does not see this blindly follows words the way a believer follows a *revelation*, not realizing that words (terms and concepts) are the threads employed by the mind to weave the net used for catching the naïve.

The egocentric mind can describe and interpret the circles of its own labyrinth, insensibly wandering through it as it creates it, but it cannot get out of this vicious cycle until it sees that it is behaving like a dog frantically chasing its own tail. And while, like a dream, wandering has no beginning nor end, insight is a sudden, current lunge out of a dream, much like an *awakening*. How and why it happens, we can never really know; but we can *awaken*.

That is why a complete philosophical system is not being offered here, but rather fragments of insights that can be used as a launch pad for the jump into freedom over the bar set by the mind. All authentic teachings are but the *pole needed to vault over the heavens*, they are but a means of bridging the illusion. However, the jumper must find his own way to use the pole to jump over the bar which his mind raises as an obstacle before every attempt at clearing the bar.

It should be borne in mind that there are no rigid rules on the Way; only rigid and unadaptable passengers. The great teacher of Chinese Zen Master Lin Chi (9th Century, the Tang Dynasty) would say to his disciples: "Donkeys are tied to posts, and people to rules. Following the rules makes you a donkey, breaking them makes you a person!"

Of course, this is not addressed to potential anarchists but rather to the wise. The wise are those who have escaped the conceptual trap laid by terms and rules. The fact that we rarely encounter them is due to our inability to recognize them; we do not recognize them because we look at the world through the lens of learned concepts and not through the eyes of innocence and because the wise use language out of the context of conformist and cultural conventions, which is the language of uncalculated spontaneity.

That is why every ego is an *arrogant fool* (although this phrase sounds like a pleonasm as every *conceited ego* is by definition *a fool*) who carries the *Wise man* on his shoulders, but keeps asking the *blind man* for the Way...

To the *Awoken* – this should be enough.

I. THE PHANTOMS OF THE INNER THEATRE

To study the Buddha Way is to study the self. To study the self is to forget the self. To forget the self is to be enlightened by the ten thousand dharmas. To be enlightened by the ten thousand dharmas is to free one's body and mind and those of others.

Dogen Zenji, founder of Japanese Soto Zen school

All these, I am quite sure, are but shadows. O Venerable Sirs! You must recognize the Man who plays with these shadows, that he is the source of all Buddhas and the refuge the followers of the Way take to wherever they may be.

Lin Chi, founder of the Lin Chi (Japanese *Rinzai*) school of Chinese Zen

I.1 Infinite beginning – the *game* that blooms from within itself

The Path of Self-Knowledge is not easily approached by those who have never set foot on it, who have never got a small taste of it. That Path is more similar to the process of artistic creation than it is to a methodical scientific process; it is more similar to spiritual meditation than it is to intellectual and theoretical abstraction.

The Path can be written about (or spoken of) in at least four ways.

From an academic distance, with an obligatory "I am distancing myself beforehand" stance, to which one may undoubtedly object: "Then why on Earth are you writing?"

Idolatrously, in awe and down on one's knees. Along with an inevitable "the Master said!" at the end of each chapter. To this one arguably may reply: "Then let the Master speak!"

Loosely preachy, rather prophetically, where instead of a title the author may write the self-advertising slogan "I told you so..." There is nothing to object to in this case. A book that offers unquestionable answers, in our humble experience, is best not opened.

Finally, from the perspective of a seeker and co-traveler, aware that we do not yet know it all and that the book we are writing opens up along with the Path we are passing through together: the reader, the author and the pen that records the traces on the covered tracks. Is there anything more exciting and more poetic than an uncertain return to the wild?

Without further ado, we invite you to take this fourth way, in the hope that together we will be able to avoid the pitfalls of the first three paths, as only the fourth of these ways is the Path.

However, the Path of Self-Knowledge is not easily approached by those who have never set foot on it, who have never got a small taste of it. That Path is more similar to the process of artistic creation than it is to a methodical scientific process; it is more similar to spiritual meditation than it is to intellectual and theoretical abstraction, because experiencing the Path goes far beyond the limits of conventional language. In order for it to continue to be transmitted, we must find a new, living, creative and original language that eludes all paralyzing conventions.

It is difficult, if not impossible, to feel, to experience the Path of Self-Knowledge in our own Being if we have not devoted a certain amount of time to meditation (self-reflection) and contemplation (self-observation) in order to reach that state of *unpretentious alertness* in which every flicker of existence, like a fallen twig or a fluttering bird, may be a trigger for immediate, intuitive insight into that primordially undivided yet omnipresent unity of life (in which we no longer distinguish between the internal and external, between ourselves and the rest of the world) and which vibrates in every atom of existence like a primordial *élan vital.*

But until he reaches this sudden insight, the seeker must go through a process of introspection (insight into the structure and dynamics of one's own mind), and self-reflection (insight into the interdependence of our *ego* and the world) in order to transcend and see through the *ego-mind* and the world and finally be brought to a certain *metaposition* in which he may leave the *ego and the world's* former state of dividedness and examine their deeper unity.

As was said, the process we go through is not scientific-technical but rather artistic and mystical. It is more similar to Ma Yuan's elegant paintings in the silence of sunken landscapes, to composing of Debussy's or Massenet's subtle *meditations,* to Saraha's concise reflexive poetry or to Emerson's essays inspired by the understated presence of the Spirit in every blink of nature.

This kind of Path is a pure immersion into an infinite stream of Consciousness, an *efflux* from which we all flow and which quenches our thirst in our passage through the desert of existence, on which we loyally return in the self-forgetfulness of creative inspiration and passion of self-knowledge, although we never really see its end in sight.

Life is a miracle only while you're a child at heart; while your consciousness is open to all the possibilities of life, while it is the consciousness of he who for the first time in his life is walking through that wondrous mystery called life. Because then, and only then, it has an infinite number of possibilities.

The cover of each new book, the door behind which a mysterious attic is hidden, the threshold of a forest in which you have never been, another human being that you have just approached – it is all one indescribable, ineffable miracle before which the heart and conscience of the child flutters like a wave in the midday breeze.

Because then he does not yet have the experiences, facts, data, memories that would fill in the covers of the unopened book, the secrecy of the attic, the opacity of the forest, the innocence of every human being... and kill the purity and splendor of the first meeting with the uncertainty of life.

Only later, with time and experience, do we lose the ability to undergo direct experience without preconceptions and projections, and life for us then ceases to be a miracle. We spend the rest of our lives looking for the irreversible wonder of the bare experience of reality in all the little things that filled our childhood, but we cannot find it because the miracle was not in the little things that we had not got over but rather in the innocence of our hearts. First we look through the *eyes of innocence*, then through the *eyes of experience* and finally through the *eyes of wisdom*.

Only when, and if, we realize this can life once more become a miracle, a miracle in which there is no need for control, manipulation, fulfilling some imposed purpose or sense of what life is supposed to be like.

Life can then be a game (which does not need a ball and two opposing teams), a game that blooms from within itself, a game that doesn't appear to have (nor need) a scenario nor a either happy or a tragic ending, a game that is one infinite beginning...

I.2 The man without a strong-point or, being rid of the ambition to be *something*

It is an imperative for the seeker on the Path to Self-Knowledge to be himself and to not imitate anything or anyone, because mimicking has never led anyone to their original condition, to his authentic Being. And whoever misses That, no matter what else he had found, has missed this path.

As long as we try to find support for our existence in something outside ourselves we will never find true security. To be self-assured, self-confident means to not be attached to anything, whose disappearance rattles our security's support. To be self-assured and self-confident is to be naked, devoid of any support, because he who does not lean on anything cannot be thrown off balance.

The path to such a *self-awareness* (in terms of integrity and self-confidence in *consciousness per se* and not in terms of egocentric self-awareness) is the path of the renunciation of all schemes and concepts, doctrines, methods and institutions which the *unsure* could rely on; for he who leans on something is nothing but a *false ego,* an ego, an actor who is aware of the instability of his mask.

It is only when we cease looking for security that we will find it, *because it is only when we stop making the effort to be something* that the authenticity for which no masks are necessary simply comes to be.

That is why it is an imperative for the seeker of the Path to Self-Knowledge to be himself and to not imitate anything or anyone, because mimicking has never led anyone to their original condition, to his authentic Being. And whoever misses That, no matter what else he had found, has missed this path.

The true I is, metaphorically speaking, an uncompromising *philosopher of the Path,* for that is the only philosophy (the path to Wisdom) that is worthy of attention; this is the only Path worth traveling. And because that Path is not tread with *the tongue nor with the rear* (that is, by verbally adopting abstract doctrines or by precisely imitating practical methods of meditation) but rather with your whole life and your entire Being.

1.3 The uprooted *I* and the world of *dead objects*

Such an I has no deeper sense of self and all his actions focus mainly on survival and on the strategic circumvention of the anxiety that transience awakens in him. The emptier it is, the more it fears its own transience. The more it fears, the more it crams its inner space with vain things, turning its life into a dusty antique shop filled with dead artefacts.

The *I* that gives up its *Self* to be accepted and thus survives, that gives up the struggle and the risk that is imminent in the struggle, is not capable of true love, which in itself is a risk and a struggle. It is afraid of the possibility of such love. As it is deprived of the personal center of its own individuality, and with it the precondition of achieving a deeper integrative center, such an *I* is as empty as a bubble.

It exists and lives in so far as it breathes. Deep passion is unattainable for it, therefore so is deep love, as well as deep pain, affection or loyalty. These are but mental abstractions to it, and periodic (impermanent) emotional reactions to them are but hysterical outbursts devoid of deeper changes in attitudes and individuality.

Such an *I* has no deeper sense of self and all his actions focus mainly on survival and on the strategic circumvention of the anxiety that transience awakens in him. The emptier it is, the more it fears its own transience. The more it fears, the more it crams its inner space with vain things, turning its life into a dusty antique shop filled with dead artefacts that are there simply to remind it that it is still alive.

And so, living and struggling to feel secure only in the world of *dead objects*, which cannot reciprocate nor deny *love*, freeing it of the anxiety that risks stir from within, such an *I* may only realize a relationship with a partner whom it treats like an object or by whom it gets treated like one. However, since an object cannot reciprocate with energy, as the capacity for passion is deeply repressed and linked to protection from the anxiety of risk, such a relationship can be no more than a short-term satisfaction and a long-term frustration, and ultimately can offer no better than a lasting and barren sense of disappointment.

Living in permanent anxiety, without any personal foundation or a strong-point, this uprooted *I* can only do three things. First, it can bow down to an external conditional morality, to religious studies or to a social worldview. Regardless of whether its origin is in a revelation, ideology or some other worldly authority, it is essential that the *uprooted* find its strong-point in another and not in itself. Second, it can turn to its Self and find support in its own, personal authenticity, in spiritual *individuality*, in a kind of moral autonomy that is unconditioned by external circumstances and authorities. And third, simply accept a *baseless existence*, existence as an endless stream of events, impressions and their experiences, living from moment to moment according to the circumstances and capacities of its own response to the challenges of the moment.

Only then can the *uprooted* live in the flow, without any restricting principles and concepts, defensive prejudices and self-justifying doctrines and theories, without external laws and conditions. Only then can he live without any remorse because he is not able to respond to the unattainable demands of self-imposed authority. Only then can he live free and at peace, navigate from wave to wave, always new and naked, fresh and *ragged from the road*, light as a fallen leaf that lets itself be carried by the omnipresent force of life and that doesn't fear being led into a storm or a wasteland...

For the *uprooted* who has surrendered to his flow, his primeval *ripple*, knows that he can no longer get lost anywhere, knowing that he has absolved and released his cargo and washed away his ambitions. And this is the most natural and also the most difficult path to *self-actualization* because it doesn't allow any bases or places of refuge on this journey on which we do not yet discern a destination.

I.4 The phantoms of the inner theatre: the *ego, non-ego and super-ego*

In such a phantom theatre, our divided ego (divided between the center of the individuality and the organizational structure itself, the architect and the construction site, the director and the cast, the controllers and the controlled) necessarily becomes a bridge between the external and the internal, the actual and the potential, the past and the future, between what we are (and do not accept) and what we want to be (and cannot).

Striving toward some *superego*, whether it be an idol, a teacher or a personalized God, is always a reflection of non-acceptance of one's own *I*. Each *ego* develops in relation to its opposite *non-ego*. To this undifferentiated, virginal wild and (un)known *non-ego*, our limited, conditioned *ego* must give a certain shape and identity (i. e. a *superego*), in order to better communicate with it, worship it, ask for its protection and guidance, and ultimately, identify with it.

However, as each *superego* is actually a phantom woven from our unconscious projections and fantasies, we can never really reach it. Therefore, it often becomes a reliable source of our frustration, complex and (self)destructive impulses. This is where the *conditioned ego*'s constant splintering and tension turn into unresolved conflicts, on one side with non-integrated *non-ego*, on the other hand with projected *superego*.

In such a phantom theatre, our *divided ego* (divided between the center of the individuality and the organizational structure itself, the architect and the construction site, the director and the cast, the controllers and the controlled) necessarily becomes a bridge between the external and the internal, the actual and the potential, the past and the future, between what we are (and do not accept) and what we want to be (and cannot).

This *I* which hasn't yet met or actualized itself, exists as a bridge between our subjective world and the world of objects through the force of circumstances and psychological relations. A bridge between them but also a crucifix, or rather fortress with a double defense: both in terms of the external requirements and the requirements of internal reality. This is the same fortress which in the end also becomes its prison, and the *ego* becomes its own captor, preventing it from recognizing that the prisoner is the king whom he bows down to.

The only way man can free himself of this dividedness is to begin to accept and to keep pace with his actual self, just as he is, without trial and judgment for these imply *conditional acceptance*. It is only with unconditional acceptance that the psychological divides within us disappear, the bridge between pseudo(worlds) becomes redundant and collapses into the abyss of its own lack of foundation, its futility so to speak.

It is only by accepting our *actual self* that we can liberate ourselves of the burden and tyranny of our *potential self*. And only when this *True Self* expresses itself as the undivided wholeness of consciousness and existence, a being so different from the *superego* (which we imagined as our ideal identity in all our frustrations and expectations) that it is unimaginable to our minds and inexpressible for our tongues.

It can only be expressed by the free, uninhibited, unpredictable, powerful flow of life through which our *actual self*, through the actualization of every moment of existence in which there are no more psychological divides. For such a *whole*, or better yet said *healed*, being, it can no longer be said that it is an *ego*, nor an *non-ego*, not a *superego*, since these phantoms of the inner theatre exist only in a reciprocal relation.

It is simply beyond all relations, and this is an experience of reality that eludes all definitions and concepts; for although the *temporary or transitional ego* is but a bridge to the other shore, it is a bridge that disappears as soon as we step onto that other shore. Furthermore, the shores and the *passer-by* who crosses over them also disappear. All that remains is the sea, and the *ripple...*

I.5 The Shadow – the *psychic reservoir* of the degraded

While this psychological divide dominates man, he cannot get what the ego loves, because his despised Shadow deprives him of the energy or power of actualization; and that which the Shadow yearns for cannot be loved by the ego as that object of desire is all that which the ego despises.

The psychological Shadow accumulates all the traits that our ego despised, whether in us or in others. All that is condemned, rejected, cut off or suppressed, all this is sludge that is accumulated by the Shadow.

This is how it becomes a living, dynamic force with unpredictable capacities for transforming as well as assuming and changing identities. It becomes somewhat of an *anti-ego* which opposes our ego at every step, sabotaging all of its idealistic, unrealistic, very much unfounded efforts.

If love is the matter at hand, the Shadow will not allow us to nurture it with the *ideal* partner, as he or she is conceived by our ego. On the contrary, the Shadow will reject our ideal just as we rejected it.

Instead of leading us towards the desired *icon*, with the indescribable force of desire (a massive repressed desire, an insatiable hunger that yearns for the light of consciousness that is its food) it drives us towards that partner who is a living embodiment of the Shadow, that is, of everything that we despised and rejected in it as in a kind of psychic reservoir.

For it is precisely through this egocentric discrimination, this self-serving trial and judgment that man divides himself into the *judge* (ego) and the *convicted* (Shadow). In this psychological divide man will not find peace until he accepts himself and the world (and our own personal world of daily life which is nothing more than a psychological projection of our Shadow) *as they are* in their natural given, without wanting to monitor and censor them, judge and punish them, correct and reeducate them.

In this psychological principle lies the meaning of Christ's evangelical message: "Judge not, lest ye be judged!" and the allegorical proverb from the Book of Genesis: "He (man) shall bruise your head, and you (snake) shall bruise his heel" (Gen. 3:15). It metaphorically suggests a deep psychological divide within the 'first man' who, due to his own egocentric delusions, was displaced from the heavenly state of unity to a state of schizophrenic split between the ego and his Shadow, shown here through the chthonic serpent symbol.

And that is why while this psychological divide dominates man, he cannot get what the ego loves, because his despised Shadow deprives him of the energy or power of actualization; and that which the Shadow yearns for cannot be loved by the ego as that object of desire is all that which the ego despises.

I.6 The revenge of the rejected Shadow

If we reject our Shadow instead of awakening it and embracing it thus integrating it, it will find a way to get revenge on us, using the incorruptible logic of the boomerang-effect to make us fatally attracted to the person that will reject, ignore and punish us, doing to us what we do to our Shadow.

Each time we are attracted to the opposite sex, this is stimulated by our psychological Shadow, which through the other person searches for a way to be sensed in the field of our consciousness and to be accepted and therefore integrated, awakened. And that is why our *better half* is chosen by our Shadow and not our *ego*. That is why we never see the person our heart choses for who he or she really is, but rather as a subtle projection of our Shadow.

But if we fall for civilization's trap (and most people do) which dictates that we must treat our Shadow (our psyche's affective-instinctive field) in a suppressing and dictatorial manner only because we are brought up to experience it as the irrational half of our being that must be controlled by our reason, we have created within ourselves un unhealthy divide and mental conflict as an ideal foundation for a lasting Hell in relationships with the opposite sex.

Namely, if we reject our Shadow instead of awakening it and embracing it thus integrating it, it will find a way to get *revenge* on us, using the incorruptible logic of the boomerang-effect to make us fatally attracted to the person that will reject, ignore and punish us, doing to us what we do to our Shadow.

The strategy for dealing with our Shadow, which was long imposed by our aggressive technology and rationalization-obsessed Western culture that is progressive when it comes to technological innovation but regressive in terms of psychological evolution, would be funny if not tragic. It is as equally absurd as if the youngest layer of our brain (the neocortex) which controls conscious, rational and voluntary actions, were to try to control much older layers such as the emotional (limbic brain) and instinctive (reptilian brain) layers of our central nervous system through repressive discipline.

Whereas knowledge and will, discipline and method sovereignly govern in the field of technology, these very strategies, roughly understood and mechanically applied, fall flat in the field of psychology. Moreover, they pave the wide and flat path to neurosis, frenzy, madness... As the conscious field of our psyche receives a small part of the total mental energy, it cannot control the psyche's larger and far more energetically powerful unconscious field. It can only learn how to expand through introspection and meditation and little by little integrate its Shadow's energy.

The concluding finale of this (re)integration process is the *awakening* or the state in which all of our mental potential is actualized, and all three parts of the psyche, all three layers of the brain function congruently and without conflicting divides. Since this is an evolutionary process that can last many lifetimes, we must do everything in our power to live, move, act and being in the *presence*.

For it is the most direct, the easiest and the shortest path to *awakening* since it doesn't tread on steep slopes, nor does it seek roundabout routes through a sort of technical bridging of psychological cracks and chasms. At the same time it is the most natural path in which the soul is cultivated just like a caring and experienced gardener cultivates his garden: he just weeds and waters the soil, leaving *nature* to do the rest.

I.7 The ego is a *Son of a bitch*, and the Shadow is his mother

Although every man is a potential Buddha inside, on the outside and in most cases, he is still a deceptive Son of a bitch who is misguided by the delusions of spiritual ignorance and who will not miss the opportunity to prove himself on the account of our naivety, if only given a chance.

Everyone's ego is *a Son of a bitch*, that's what anyone who dares enter into a clinch with it needs to realize, otherwise they will end up on their backs, defeated, broken and crushed, before even realizing whom they were dealing with. When we first clearly see where things stand with our own ego, it will be easier to figure out how to deal with the ego of another man.

Although all religions teach us that every human being has an ultimate spiritual nature filled with wisdom, love and righteousness, in practice we should not be so naive as to forget that every unenlightened man also has an ego which stands as a veil of ignorance over the smoldering lights of his yet unawakened True Nature. In other words, although every man is a potential Buddha inside, on the outside and in most cases, he is still a deceptive *Son of a bitch* who is misguided by the delusions of spiritual ignorance and who will not miss the opportunity to prove himself on the account of our naivety, if only given a chance.

You might ask why we are so averse to the nature and character of His Majesty *Ego*. Therefore we will explain: Every ego is a *Son of a bitch*, whether he admits it himself or not, because each ego has his psychological *Shadow* for a mother. And the *Shadow* is like a vast reservoir, it stores all of our irrational and creative forces, our inherited instincts but also our socially conditioned emotions, rejected and scorned, repressed or hidden traits that naturally and spontaneously tend to manifest and actualize themselves in the conscious field of the psyche. And in order to realize its natural tendency, it will use detours and collateral paths if its direct roads are blocked or cut off.

It will flirt, seduce, blackmail, trade, threaten, manipulate, try all the possible epic and dramatic roles that are available to it, from Aeschylus through Shakespeare to Beckett. In brief, it will pimp and prostitute itself in this tragicomic theater of the absurd, only to affirm itself under "the spotlight", just to get out of the *psychological underworld* which it was condemned to without an appeal, to which it was exiled without the possibility of an impeachment.

Now we may ask ourselves: "And what role does Mr. Ego have in this *theatre of shadows?*" Briefly put, the Shadow is a prostitute and the ego her procurer. Or more explicitly, the Ego is a saprophyte grown from the *psychological humus* of the Shadow. They always go hand in hand, like the heads and tails of an illusion. In a way the Ego is both her *Pygmalion* and her creation, her most subtle, most sophisticated creation, so 'unreal' that it is elusive, like the moon reflected on the dark, undulating surface of a lake.

Despite this (or perhaps due to it) he is her omnipresent producer and promoter, in the virtual world which is a figment of the imagination of that inexhaustibly creative *Shadow*. Their relationship is a mere trade (the principle that underpins most unawakened interpersonal relationships) between the lame and the blind. He points her in the right direction, and she carries him on her shoulders. For the ego cannot function or survive without the Shadow's energy that nourishes and sustains it, and the Shadow without the ego is like traveling without a compass, because the ego at least temporarily gives her that *transitive center* (albeit limited and rather myopic) until the real *center of consciousness* is not awakened or unveiled.

If we look at the manifestation of this principle from a broader supra-individual perspective, we will see that the ambiguity of this relationship is reflected in each relation between two human beings. The ego accepts the other as a partner if its Shadow provides the necessary energy. Then it is willing to tolerate the other person's *ego* insomuch as the delivery or exchange of energy is equivalent to the 'tolerance' that the ego must endure. When the exchange is no longer adequate, when the energy source is exhausted or when the partner's Shadow begins to fail to provide its energy, the ego then turns to new energy *resources*.

Like a true *Son of a bitch* the ego is self-sufficient. It is permanently attached to no one. In its narcissistic dream in which it alone is real and eternal and everyone else (even the whole world) is transient and illusory, there is no room for deep love and real relationships. His life is a struggle for power and competition for dominance, because this is the only way it can confirm itself, providing itself with the necessary energy and prolonging its fragile existence over and over again.

All up until one unexpected moment, the one it will not be able to control and manipulate, the moment of Awakening.

II. WHO IS A PHANTOM DRAGGING ITS CORPSE AROUND

Chit (universal consciousness) itself, descending from the stage of cetana, becomes chitta (individual consciousness), inasmuch as it becomes contracted in conformity with the object of consciousness.

Ksemaraja: Pratyabhijnahrdayam (The Heart of the doctrine of Self-recognition), the central text in Kashmir Shaivism

Everything is a manifestation of the Buddha-nature, which is not defiled in passions or purified in enlightenment. It is above all categories. If you want to see the nature of your being, free your mind from thoughts of reality and you will see by yourself its serenity and its plenitude of life.

Hui Neng, the Sixth Patriarch and most important reformer of Zen Buddhism

II.1 The ego – a dream from which we can(not) wake!?

The ego is just a dream, but it is a dream that we keep/support with our unconscious. And the unconscious is a matrix that generates all forms of addictions: to drugs, alcohol, sex, one's career, gambling... For addiction is nothing but a form of psy-

chological reductionism that necessarily is the cause of the ego's tyranny in our spiritual life

The ego is an imaginary structure, a mental cocoon woven from our impressions, memories, premeditations, concepts... This structure is a densely woven net, like crystal cobwebs, in which our True Being longingly pupates, like a butterfly with undeveloped wings.

As long as we are not able to see the subtle psychological weave which draws energy from our whole being in order to keep itself alive, we will languish as its prisoners. We will live, work, breathe, feel, think of nothing else but being able to feed that phantom with our energy, that *exhausting dream* from which we cannot wake up, all until we are able to recognize its eeriness.

In short, the ego is just a dream, but it is a dream that we keep/support with our unconscious. And the unconscious is a matrix that generates all forms of addictions: to drugs, alcohol, sex, one's career, gambling... for addiction is nothing but a form of psychological reductionism that is necessarily the cause of the ego's tyranny in our spiritual life. How can that neurotic reductionism reduce such a rich array of features that are hidden in the entirety of spiritual life to one or more fixations and a number of supporting elementary life functions?

To the man who has not awakened or integrated his *spiritual core* or True Being into his entire spiritual life (and therefore not actualized it), life is too intricate for him to adequately meet its complex requirements. Therefore, he seeks an extrinsic *omnipotent axis*, around which he seeks to focus and organize his psychophysical integrity. However, life teaches us at every step that there is no extrinsic axis that may substitute and replace the internal core; and such a shaky, artificially organized *integrity* constantly faces life's serious trials that it is not able to cope with.

This is how one becomes addicted to various *mental prostheses* and substitutes (regardless of whether it is alcohol, drugs, sex, money, fame or social status), while searching for the artificial *center* of our ever so fragile, unstable and fleeting existence which the life without a genuine internal identity spends quickly and relentlessly for a mere trifle... leaving behind a stranded mental ruin which tries to find its lost personal balance in clinics that treat depression and neuroses and in institutions that "get" you off drugs and alcohol.

And as if by some unwritten formula, the more abstract and illusory a man's *pseudo-support* is, the more unstable the mental focus of his existence and the stronger his dependence on artificial substitutes is. There is no way out of this vicious, somnambulistic circle until man goes in search of the inner core, the core of his own Being.

And this is an entirely different organization (or rather, integration) of individuality, consciousness and life... This is the *Path*.

II.2 Forgetting one*self* means unconditionally accepting one's Self

And this is possible for one simple reason: because the one who accepts without any conditions is in fact our True Being, while the one who sets conditions, who tries and discards is our selfish, pathetic, small pseudo-self.

There is nothing man will not turn to in order to run away from him*self*: opiates, ambitions, achievements, ideals, ideologies, religions, collecting titles, status symbols and goods... Man will turn the world, oceans and sky upside down, in order to drift into *self-forgetfulness.* But he cannot succeed until he sees through the paradox: that the only path to self-forgetfulness is to unconditionally accept one's Self, with *no ifs, or buts*!

And this is possible for one simple reason: because *the one who accepts without any conditions* is in fact our True Being, while the one who sets conditions, who tries and discards is our selfish, pathetic, small *pseudo-self.*

When there no longer are any conditions, there also no longer are any internal divides, no repression from imposter judges and investigators whose omnipresence, like a nightmare drove us to continuing, painful, egocentric *self-consciousness.* When everything is accepted unreservedly, we can let the *controller* rest in peace; we can sink the *false* into self-forgetfulness and rise in the awakening of our True Being.

This True Nature which all beings have (for lack of a more precise term, the metaphor employed by Buddhists, Vedantists and Shaivites shall be used) is called *self-illuminating or self-mirroring Consciousness* because all beings, phenomena and conditions – only reflections of its attributes – are in the mirror of this creation. And Its attributes are countless, as are phenomena and beings. That is why that *eternally awakened consciousness* is the center of all states. It is both the light that illuminates phenomena and conditions and the mirror that reflects but does not adopt or retain them.

It is omnipresent and all-pervasive in its unconditionality. If it is not as such, we will never achieve it; and if it is, we could never have lost it to begin with. Its presence can be experienced, actualized, made present right now only if we allow our own, individual consciousness to dismiss all concepts, blurring ideas and discriminatory views.

This presence is the only Path to the Awakening. It is looking without differentiation and correction, which creates a key prerequisite for *contemplation* or seeing with the whole, undivided being, a spontaneous act in which instincts, senses and emotions as well as reason and intellect are simultaneously and coherently coordinated in a deeper center of consciousness, which for want of a better term we will call *intuition (prajna)*.

Simply put, *seeing with the entire being* is nothing more than *being present* and allowing the entire universe (and consciousness and its phenomena) to balance itself out in this presence, *mirroring itself,* with no middlemen, no controllers, no navigators. And this is the natural path to the return to our True Nature and at the same time to its spontaneous self-pronouncement/self-mirroring...

II.3 *The ego* as reference center of all relations or center of the circumference-less circle

The mind and the ego relate to each other the same way a circle and its center do. The circle exists only in relation to its center, and the center only exists in relation to the circle. From the perspective of individual consciousness, the ego is the center that has gathered a cluster of mental content (that support the idea of an isolated individuality) around itself and consequently has accumulated the necessary mental energy that will serve as a protective cocoon.

In freedom's infinite space which is, right before us, opened up by a Consciousness that is unrelated to its state, the *ego* exist only as a reference center for the differentiating forces of attraction and repulsion of certain states. And each individual state is differentiated from faceless, pulsating mental potentiality, like an *ego* in relation to other states, which it defines as a *non-ego*.

In reality, the *ego* and the *non-ego* are but the abstract relationship points of differentiated mental states, and they last as long as the relationships do. That's why the ego cannot survive without relationships and relations. However, since Consciousness is infinitely undifferentiated, *a circle with no circumference,* each point of the relationship or differentiation (a wave that had risen and picked a calm ocean surface) may be one center of the infinite circle. If we consider the *panpsychic* reality from this perspective, the question "Is the True Nature the ego or the non-ego?" becomes superfluous.

The mind and the *ego* relate to each other the same way a circle and its center do. The circle exists only in relation to its center, and the center only exists in relation to the circle. From the perspective of individual consciousness, the *ego* is the center that has gathered a cluster of mental content (that support the idea of an isolated individuality) around itself and consequently has accumulated the necessary mental energy that will serve as a protective cocoon.

This is a two-layer cocoon because it has a protective function, both from the external, physical world and from the inner, psychic world. And the *ego* as the center of the circle is the *controller* who at times opens the doors to the outside and at other times opens the doors to the inside.

But from the perspective of the awakened consciousness, the *ego* is but a short-term isolated wave of infinite undifferentiated consciousness that is in itself a *circle with no circumference*, a ripple with no coast. In it, each being can be a center, but then it is automatically separated from other beings, as well as from the source of the original unity with the undivided Consciousness.

When a being lives *just as so*, not experiencing itself as a center, but rather modestly allowing the Whole to become clear through it, like an endless ocean through a wave, through a vibration, a moment, through the shower of infinite existence, then there are no longer any divides, no need for a protective cocoon and consequently no need for a circle or a pseudo--center.

The individual mind without an *ego-center* is not a closed but an *open circle*, which constantly spills over from countless other areas of life and never stops flowing, like the unharnesssed current of *unlimited Consciousness*, evading the shores of (self)deceiving divides. And the seemingly isolated mental energy, in these deep insights, lives free and has returned to its primordial nature, non-adhesive Awakeness.

II.4 Unmasking the Great Illusionist by refusing to pay him any attention

Based on that experience we can directly see that the world and mind are one in their essence, though functioning as two aspects of the same illusion. Mind is a Great Illusionist who draws this world of countless phenomena from his pocket (or hat, as you like it) like a skilled magician. Our true Self stands at the base of mind/world – as a beacon shedding the light at their activity but does not identify with the magic of the Great Illusionist.

Creating and maintaining *the picture of me and the world* depends on the continuity of the mind in action and our attention included in building the mind's castles in the sand. Ego (which is not some passing echo anymore of interference between an individual mind and universal Consciousness) and mind exist only because of continuity of thinking. When consciousness is withdrawn from the interaction with thoughts and objects, world, mind and ego disappear – and only the eternal testifying and self-reflecting consciousness of the Self remains.

We know that a person who is not used to a disciplined meditation practice and unconscious of living in a branched matrix of mind, finds it hard to understand and even harder to accept. Moreover, it is almost impossible to find precise words to describe this experience at least to a certain extent to someone who has never had this experience before. However, to the one who has systematically done a chosen meditation practice and managed to dive deeply into contemplation, it is possible to experience this basic condition of our consciousness which transcends thought. Vedanta and Yoga describe this condition as *passive witnessing*, and Vijnana-vada school as the condition of *mirroring consciousness*.

While diving within, a practicioner arrives to that level – and he only experiences that basic timeless condition – *I am* (aham). This is the basis for the possibility of all potential conditions that can emerge from it any moment, as soon as mind moves from its static centre where it temporarily became still and quiet. Naturally, since the nature of mind is energy, and the nature of energy is movement – after its stillness phase, mind will start moving again, and together with it, there will appear this world as the creation of the mind, together with all countless attributes and phenomena as their reflections.

Based on that experience we can directly see that the world and mind are one in their essence, though functioning as two aspects of the same illusion. Mind is a Great Illusionist who draws this world of countless phenomena from his pocket (or hat, as you like it) like a skilled magician. Our true Self stands at the base of mind/world – as a beacon shedding the light at their activity but does not identify with the *magic* of the Great Illusionist.

More vividly described, in their relationship the conscious Self functions as a *basis* on a stretched framed canvas, and the mind as a leading thread or *weft* which weaves a dynamic tapestry we call – creation. This incessant game of creation and dissolution of the world of illusions (which Hinduists metaphorically describe as a playful dance of – Shiva Nataraja, the Lord of the dance) is natural and spontaneous, and does not need any intellectual interpretation or mind control.

However, the nature of ego, which for survival uses mind in order to build its own virtual and parallel reality – creates a mental labyrinth that serves as its own prison. Chained by defense structures of ego, mind is not capable of transcending it as long as it believes ego is something – real. Therefore, encouraging messages like: *Cast away your ego!*, *Let go of your ego!*, *Transcend your ego!*, work exactly like what their sound – contradictory and counterproductive.

How can cast away ego *the one* who finds it real? How can cast away ego the one who, with the effort to let it go, still includes it in his *reality*? How can transcend ego the one who sees it as an obstacle? It is a paradox, the more one makes an effort to overcome ego, the more it grows as a bigger, more insurmountable obstacle, fed by his own ambition.

The only way out from this *noose with a double knot* is not to include the energy of conscious attention in the process of self-preserving and self-confirming ego, that uses drama and burlesque to attract our attention and depletes our energy in order to continue its misleading games. In other words, ego is like a mechanical restless wheel that constantly *draws water to its own mill.*

As during an entire day an average person is unconsciously absorbed and drawn into ego's games, and during the night continues to be a slave to his dreams, conscious refusal to give ego's games our attention is possible by meditative shift of our attention to *contained self-observation* devoid of interpreting and conceptualization of one's experience. Then, everything that through a sieve of self-observation comes out of automatic, unconscious millstone of ego-recycling, becomes cleared and reintegrated into the force of pure consciousness or presence.

Thus, ego is naturally peeled by itself through simple withdrawal of attention to *His Majesty the Great Illusionist's* tricks and games, until what is left of it in the end and what it actually is – *a heap of peelings.*

II.5 The Great Master of All Illusion

The greatest mystery under the heavens is the following question: How does that phantom entity survive? That phantom which is not this body, nor these senses, nor this mind, nor all possible identities, which with ease and with no feeling of guilt he changes like an actor changes the masks, like a puppeteer changes the puppets which our deeper I very well knows are nothing more than disguises and figments of the imagination.

Man's central delusion, from which all other self-delusion arise, is that his *conditioned ego* is true, monolithic, *organic* so to say, while the ego in fact is not a kind of separate center, a kind of permanent entity or quality.

It is just our consciousness's ability to identify with the identities that the mind constantly creates. And so the mind and ego function as two sides of a coin, two wheels coming from the same illusion mechanism, mutually supporting themselves like the seductive *Maya* and the vanity-misled *Narcissus*.

But this game can only last as long as our True Being does not awaken and see through that false, illusory drama. This can only be loosely said, as our True Being is always awoken; only we, in all our somnambulistic fantasies, are not aware of it. However, once we do become aware of this, once we are startled out of this reverie, we cease to identify with the offered identities and the ego, which cannot survive without an identity, dissipates like a nighttime phantom in the light of dawn.

The greatest mystery under the heavens is the following question: *How does that phantom entity survive?* That phantom which is not this body, nor these senses, nor this mind, nor all possible identities, which with ease and with no feeling of guilt he changes like an actor changes the masks, like a puppeteer changes the puppets which our deeper I very well knows are nothing more than disguises and figments of the imagination.

What is and how was woven that spider's web, invisible yet difficult to break, that the invisible *web Dragon*, that self-recycling reptile woven from the shadows of all discarded disguises, constantly tries to clutch onto like on a salutary blade? What *steel, mercury or flame* was this web woven from, that web on which the whole universe of illusion is left hanging? The web that gives it the certainty that despite all the mimicry and transformations, despite the chaos of all the seals and supports, it can say of itself with unruffled self-confidence that indisputably self-empowering *I*; even though he never got to intimately know who and what is that *self-proclaimed I*. But the *phantom* does not worry about such trifles. The only thing that is important to this indestructible being is that it continues its phantom dance.

However, if in at least one, lightning-fast flash we manage to perceive the *ego's* eerie insubstantiality, then it is also possible to perceive the mind from a completely different perspective, in a totally different light: as a structure knitted from countless concepts and self-defence strategies, like a web that offered false refuge in its cocoon but in reality kept us in the dungeon of self-delusion, not allowing us to hatch out and fly away to meet our true nature, *freedom*.

But this freedom cannot be achieved with new doctrines, methods and techniques that attempt to disempower the *ego-mind* strategy. This freedom can blossom only from presence, from the life that is presence from step to step. Only that kind of life can snatch dominance and energy away from the egocentric mind. And once it is cut off from the continuous flow of energy that is provided by our attention (which is enchanted and seduced by its misleading game) the mind begins to dissolve, the psychic structure that built it begins to disintegrate, and the ego that it appointed as the ruler of its enchanted *Camelot* begins to fade away... And then the entire previous life that was under the guidance and control of the Grand Master of Illusion will begin to be revealed as one big farce.

What remains in the end? An open space, a bare land, a windy land through which consciousness's liberated forces dispel the last remains of the web. At first there is a feeling of loneliness, of not belonging, of being purposeless... Then there is a greater development and blossoming of the inner fulfilment that only independence from all conditionality and freedom from all illusions can offer.

II.6 The idol of all idols and surrogate of all surrogates

Until the 'self-image' is disempowered, man cannot be liberated from the tyranny of the ego because that 'narcissistic image' is the idol that pulls man's mental energy outwards and projects it into the world of projection, instead of turning it towards the center of the True Being or Self.

The ego is an *empty bubble*, but it keeps itself alive by feeding on the unawakened, unintegrated contents of the unconscious. The ego has no shape, but like a chameleon it is able to identify with every shape that at a given moment suits him or is necessary to him. The ego has no face, but like Narcissus it is in love with its own image and deadly aggressive towards everything that distorts that image, towards everything that he cannot control in order to preserve his blind adoration's idol, *His Majesty the I.*

The ego cannot exist without his idol whom he bows down and who is the purpose of his existence. That is why the egocentric can destroy themselves when their idol is dethroned, because they did not find a deeper strong-point in their own being. The ego has no steady attributes, but his job is to constantly judge and discriminate against other people's qualities; by accepting those who are suitable to its narcissistic image and rejecting those who are unsuitable to it.

Such a strategy creates a painful split between the accepted and rejected part of the self in human beings, which in turn creates a fertile ground for the ongoing internal conflict in the human psyche that is the cause to many neuroses, all until this conflict becomes awakened and releases itself in such a way that the *rejected ego* is accepted and integrated.

All this shows that the ego, although it is in its essence an empty soap bubble, is capable of taking on different forms and developing various deception strategies, against its environment as well as against itself, in order to preserve its narcissistic self-image. Therefore, until the 'self-image' is disempowered, man cannot be freed from the tyranny of the ego, because that 'narcissistic image' is the idol that pulls man's mental energy outwards and projects it into the world of projection instead of turning it towards the center of the True Being or Self.

That is why the *idol* must be dispossessed in order for the searcher to find the source of life, creativity and cognitive potential or its true Self. He who does not search for the Source inevitably turns to worshiping surrogates, and what is the ego but the idol of all idols, the surrogate of all surrogates?

II.7 Who is the *phantom* dragging its corpse around?

This game is much more subtle than the one in which person Gama consciously deceives the world around him, posing to be someone he in fact is not. The matter at hand here is primordial illusions through which person Gamma unconsciously deceives himself, like an actor who, by changing roles so often, forgets his true identity.

The problem with the *phantom* (technically, the ego) is not just that it is a *false personality*, that it is a *person Gama* who is wrongfully impersonating *Mr. Beta*. The problem is much more serious. For it is easy to see that person Gama is not the *gentleman* he is pretending to be. All masks fall sooner or later. All actors are seen through sooner or later. And what then? When he is exposed, person Gama will exchange one mask, one role, for another. And so the game continues.

However, this game is much more subtle than the one in which person Gama consciously deceives the world around him, posing to be someone he in fact is not. The matter at hand here is primordial illusions through which person Gamma unconsciously deceives himself, like an actor who, by changing roles so often, forgets his true identity.

In such a state and circumstances, *Mr. Beta* is not but one of the roles that will disappear from the stage the moment the actor takes off his costume. No, he continues the autonomous game like an unreal, *imaginary phantom* who does not exist in principle but who in practice successfully sells himself to his surroundings for a *living man*.

This is a *phantom*, who had never really "risen from the grave", that drags the *possessed* mind/body around like a corpse. This is the *made-up identity* that we have imagined like a child that has wandered into a dark forest who has invented an imaginary friend in order to take courage. But when he finds his way out of the forest and returns to his home, that very same moment he forgets his *imaginary companion*.

But, it seems that it is much more dangerous for the seemingly adult to have an imaginary friend because if the problem is not detected in time, it takes root in psychotic depths.

Namely, most people so unquestionably identify with their "imaginary double" that they never consider that behind the layers of that phantasy, a more essential and persistent identity than that of this *cabaret actor's* might be watching over them.

Unfortunately, forgetting his True Self, man invests all his mental powers and passions of the heart, even his bone marrow, in maintaining that *phantom*, much like he invests in his life savings or in his life long guarantor. But *He* survives despite his illusoriness precisely because he feeds off our mental powers, off our heart's endeavors, off our *spinal marrow*.

How come then does *He* not take all that we have given him, like a mad gambler placing a deposit on something *unseen*, convinced that *He* is all that we are and all that we have? And so that *phantom* of ours sucks on us like a parasite, like a creeper, like a nightmare, hour after hour, day after day, for years, until the last breath.

He who was never alive, *He* who is the ghost that has risen from the grave of our *suppressed I*, *He* cannot bear life nor anything that is actually alive. And that *phantom* will trample and destroy us to the agony of death if we do not invest all our spiritual strength in disempowering and overthrowing him like an intruder or parasite in the dust of illusion which he hatched from. For despite his tenacious resistance, which is inconceivable for an illusion woven of dreams, that *ghost* feels disconsolately empty and never reveals that the whole world is not enough to fill him and make him alive.

And so, whoever does not stand in the Truth, in his *I am*, lives, withers and dies in the shadow of dreams, lies and illusions. And the path will be futile to him, no matter how long it is, because he is just going in circles... until he awakens.

III. FROM DEAD MECHANISM TO LIVING *SELF*

A considerable percentage of the people we meet on the street are people who are empty inside, that is, they are actually already dead. It is fortunate for us that we do not see and do not know it. If we knew what a number of people are actually dead and what a number of these dead people govern our lives, we should go mad with horror.

G. I. Gurdjieff, Russian mystic and spiritual teacher

The 'I' in its purity is experienced in intervals between the two states or two thoughts. Ego is like the caterpillar which leaves its hold only after catching another. Its true nature can be found when it is out of contact with objects or thoughts.

Ramana Maharshi, modern Advaita Vedanta teacher

III.1 The consciousness between observation and action – two faces of a hollow medallion

When through persistent meditation we investigate both observer and performer, we will grasp the essence of both, the two faces of a hollow medallion. For in this inaction and ripple Consciousness reflects the observation and the action, but the observers and the movers of this magnificent cosmic game are nowhere to be found.

The abundant world of beings is but the imprint of countless forms in a unique and universal Consciousness. In reality there is nothing but that universal Consciousness and the abundance of forms in which it manifests itself and hides (*Avarana*) its true nature.

The moment when consciousness that is limited by the form that it creates identifies with that very form is the moment when the *individual I* (ego) is born. Who is it then that divides that single, universal Consciousness into a number of functions: stimulation, perception, memory (or the accumulation of impressions), desire, feeling, thoughts? Who is it that closes that series of the consciousness's functions in a linking chain, which through the innate cultural custom of categorizing and cataloging everything we wrongly identify as the umbrella term "*mind*"?

It is not necessary to point out that this *fanatical registrar* is our ego. Thanks to the consciousness's distribution into its functions and to its static and dynamic aspect, the ego tries to subject it to its own control and interests. The conscious, subconscious, unconscious; potential, latent, actual – these are the ego's creations whose motto can be boiled down to that frequently cited Roman maxim: *Divide and rule!*

It is by using this strategy that the divider becomes the main obstacle between form and consciousness, single being and universe, the being and the Self. It is only thanks to the ego that the universal Consciousness is reduced to the individual mind, which is further divided into the 6 mentioned functions and 3 states (waking consciousness, dreaming, and dreamless sleep) which correspond to the three levels (the conscious, the subconscious, the unconscious) of one's consciousness.

It is only thanks to this discriminative center (which Buddhists call *manas*, Hindus call *ahamkara* and Westerners call *ego*) that the primordial Oneness is revealed to us as multitude, and the original undivided Being as a universe of innumerable differentiated phenomena; although all forms are nothing but a shadow on a clean mirror, but imprints in consciousness's energy, retained for as long as the ego's personal memory lasts. This memory can last for several decades, even a century for the individual *ego*, but it is an exceedingly brief flash in universal Consciousness's mirror that exists beyond the mind and time.

For consciousness is like an endless wave that flows from the state of inaction and observation to the state of action and creation, and back again. For the *untarnished center* of that universal Consciousness, call it God, Brahman or Buddha, that waves rises and falls lightning-fast like the blink of Brahma's eye. But for countless creatures that ripple in the foam of that wave that blink lasts a lifetime.

While consciousness is inert and contemplates (self-mirrors) from within, the universe, abundance and ego are but a possibility. When consciousness gets going and creates a form (and in doing so identifies with it, as the form cannot survive a second longer than the identification lasts because this identification is the investment of energy in the given form) the universe (space-time-mind) the abundance of forms and the ego simultaneously appear. But as soon as the universal Consciousness withdraws from the game of creation into a state of inaction and quiet, it pulls all creations with all their potential into a state of latency.

When we realize this, though it only be for a moment, how could we call the universe, abundance and the ego, real? How can we possibly understand them as being anything more than God's game? What can a final, absolute *reality* be besides the alternation between the inaction and the ripple of the infinite ocean of Consciousness!

When through persistent meditation we investigate both observers and performers, we will grasp the essence of both, the two faces of a hollow medallion. For in this inaction and ripple Consciousness reflects the observation and the action, but the observers and the movers of this magnificent cosmic game are nowhere to be found.

III.2 Essence and Personality
as light and screen

The mystery of the gradual disclosure of our True Being lies in their mutual relationship. Because Essence cannot be developped, it can only be uncovered. It is personality that can be developed, but only insofar as all that is superfluous drops away from it in the process of development, everything that the social superego has grafted on it, so that eventually through it our essential, authentic I may spontaneously be revealed.

Renowned spiritual teacher from the last century George Ivanovich Gurdjieff, founder of the Fourth Way School and Institute for the Harmonious Development of Man, in his teachings constantly emphasized the difference between the Essence and personality of the man.

It is relatively easy to explain in words that Essence is our true, innate and immutable nature, whereas personality is the mindset that we have acquired and organized under the influence of education, culture and tradition. So it is an external, mental *installation* that has nothing in common with our True Being, but systematically carries out repression on us in order to break us, deplete the core of life from us and mold us in a dead stencil that is more appropriate to its ambitions and hunger for the social prestige that modern civilization so relentlessly dictates as the irreplaceable goal and purpose of human life.

However, it is much more difficult to experience and become aware of the distinction between Essence and personality. This is the *prestigious* life assignment of each personal, which cannot be carried out by anyone except himself. Sometimes all that is necessary is a sudden tide of inspiration which raises us to a higher level of perception and gives us insight. But this is a very rare occurrence, unless it is karmically deserved or bestowed by the mercy of an accomplished teacher. Most often, for such a profound insight, we have to go through the time-consuming, laborious and uncertain process of meditation, and even then liberating insight is not guaranteed.

So it is worth saying something about this, simply as stimulus for the seeker of the Path to persevere in the effort of self-knowledge. In the mature and balanced personal, Essence and personality are not mutually exclusive but rather cooperate in weaving the *tapestry of life* as a basis and weft. Personality follows Essence like a shadow, and Essence supports personality as its foundation. Personality is indispensable to Essence in order for the latter to be displayed in the external world through the former, and Essence is vital to personality because without it as a foundation personality cannot develop. The mystery of the gradual disclosure of our True Being lies in their mutual relationship.

Because Essence cannot be developed, it can only be uncovered. It is personality that can be developed, but only insofar as all that is superfluous drops away from it in the process of development, everything that the social *superego* has grafted on it, so that eventually through it our essential, *authentic I* may spontaneously be revealed.

When all the circumstances for the revelation of our *authentic I* have matured, personality's screen, which had up until then overshadowed the Self's light of awareness and facilitated its gradual disclosure, becomes redundant and Essence is then disclosed in its fullness. This process is called the awakening of the True Self. It is important to realize that transcending personality is not a matter of rejection, but rather of development and "dropping off". And the realization of essence is not an achievement but rather an awakening, the revelation and the dawn of that which we had never lost.

The wisdom and art of liberating oneself from the conflicts within and tyranny of the hypertrophied personality lie in exposing its egocentric, chameleon-like masks and games in order for it to be restrained and for its activities to be refocused on the sole reason it exists, and that is to uncover and manifest the true Self.

III.3 The root of ignorance and suffering is in the oblivion of the True Self

The root of self-forgetfulness, that is, the cause of and manner of reaching self-forgetfulness, cannot be determined with certainty, but we can recall the True Self and thus free ourselves of ignorance and suffering. The development of consciousness and devotion through meditation (reflection) and contemplation (observation), concisely and metaphorically, are the two wings of the bird of enlightenment.

The root of all the countless forms of human suffering is in universal spiritual ignorance (*avidya*). The root of ignorance is in the oblivion of the True Being or Self. The root of self-forgetfulness, that is, the cause of and manner of reaching self--forgetfulness, cannot be determined with certainty, but we can recall the True Self and thus free ourselves of ignorance and suffering.

There are many methods of awakening from the dream of self-forgetfulness but it all ultimately comes down to the two most direct methods:

I. The development of *consciousness* through the exploration of our True Nature by asking the question: "*Who am I?*" (Koham)

II. The development of *devotion* by confirming the true Self through an unreserved identification with the Supreme Self: "*I am He!*" (Soham).

Simply put, the development of consciousness and devotion through meditation (reflection) and contemplation (observation), concisely and metaphorically, *are the bird of enlightenment's two wings.*

On the path to awakening, every searcher, at a mature level of self-development, should come to understand several important principles.

First, that each person in its essence is perfect, only he or she has not become aware of that yet.

Second, that through the experience of life, each person develops its individuality precisely in order to gradually awaken its perfection. This experience is the Path of Self-Knowledge, and living conditions and the number of different incarnations through which we pass are but good or bad *schools of self-development* through which we must pass in order to awaken/enlighten our True Self.

Third, the development of an individuality that gradually enlightens and integrates all the qualities of the person must primarily be reflected through:

- the breadth of our consciousness
- the depth of our empathy and
- the persistence of our authenticity.

This experience is the development of *wisdom and virtue.*

Wisdom and virtue mutually support themselves on the Path to Self-Knowledge (which all classical schools of self-development knew and cherished) as the left and right hand during the thorny climb up the *tree of knowledge,* back to Paradise Lost.

Although today many of the modern schools of self-development offer a number of shortcuts and weekend workshops to *instant enlightenment* (often supported by the would-be *scientific proof* of irresponsible success-mongers that pass for *scientists*) to the honest and patient seeker on this path, life will eventually prove that there is no other Path.

III.4 From dead mechanism to living Self

The disciplined training of consciousness or a type of life shock is required in order for man to realize that his mechanical behavior is the unconscious response to his environment's presumed expectations, which he has adopted as his own inner imperative.

The unconscious man behaves like a set mechanism. He is a prisoner to the given attributes of the body and the mind, which are actuated by mechanically conditioned instinctive and hereditary-educational models.

The unconscious man is simply "possessed" with this *artificial structure* as some foreign, installed mechanism which he is not able to handle; he does not know how to behave with it, nor does he know how to behave with the body and mind's the often conflicting tendencies. The pseudo-center or *conditioned ego* should control, balance and handle this half-biological, half socio-psychological mechanism, but it simply is not able to do so because it itself is an inseparable part of the installed system.

The disciplined training of consciousness or a type of life shock is required in order for man to realize that his mechanical behavior is the unconscious response to his environment's presumed expectations, which he has adopted as his own inner imperative. Furthermore, when man dives into meditation deep enough, when he goes beyond the curtain which is created by the activities of the mind-body, he will find that the existence of the ego-center in his essence is a pure fantasy. However, this cannot be explained with words, this must be experienced in meditation, for it is only through direct insight that we can achieve understanding and liberation.

How then can we get out of this rigged system which we have partly inherited through biological-genetic means, and partly adopted during adulthood through education and the influence of our socio-cultural environment? Based on practical research and personal experiences, we believe that the most direct route to the departure from an unconscious, mechanical life is to let our egocentric will for self-preservation and self-affirmation, which arises from incorrect formation of the *conditioned ego*, to give in to our true center or Self.

It is only when we stabilize ourselves in our true Self that we become able to balance, handle and use this *body-mind mechanism* with which we had previously wrongfully and ignorantly identified. Then our pseudo-center becomes redundant so it can naturally dry out and fall off.

For the *formation of the ego* never was the permanent goal and purpose of our overall development. The purpose of the formation of that *transitional center* was for it to simply serve as a temporary bridge in the development from the unconscious-mechanical to the conscious-spiritual life, from a benumbed, slumbering mechanism to a live, awakened Self.

Therefore, we should not disregard the ego's role. It is simply one phase that has its own function in this transitional process. The problem arises when your True Being is replaced by it because a properly cultivated and directed *temporary ego* can functionally serve to improve the development process, while a *wild I above all*, grown on fallacious uncultivated bases, creates great confusion and suffering. A great teacher or great pain is needed, often both, to cleanse, transform and retrain it into building the bridge to True Being.

III.5 The split *ego* and the fatal attraction of the *Unconscious*

Over time, the more man becomes aware of that split and of the dire consequences of a refusal to accept it, the more he becomes attracted to consciousness's opposite magnetic pole, the being's essence or Self.

Man is born split, separated from his essence, from his True Nature. And the deeper this split is, the greater the pain of this separation is, the stronger his desire for self-forgetfulness in merging with the unconscious (or better said unawakened) half of his psyche is.

Stemming from this desire is fatal attraction to drugs, sexuality devoid of emotion, aggressive demonstrations of power, flirtation with (self)destruction; in other words, all those agents that provide man with the short-term ability to separate himself from the unbearable tyranny of the *split ego* and free-fall into the illusory happiness of unconscious. But that happiness is never permanent. It briefly stuns the mind and blunts its critical edge, but in the long run it exhausts the limited supplies of energy and consciousness which are available to the *ambivalent ego*, transforming man into a psychophysical wreck.

Over time, the more man becomes aware of that split and of the dire consequences of a refusal to accept it, the more he becomes attracted to consciousness's opposite magnetic pole, the being's essence or Self. That is when mental energy's flux instead of flowing downstream goes upstream, and thus begins man's battle to wrestle himself away from the ruinous attraction to the unconscious and find true serenity and fulfillment in conscious life. And that means to dwell in the *center*, in the spiritual heart, in our Original undivided Being.

This *upstream* flux to the return to the Source is hard and long, full of pitfalls and temptations. For man to be able to last out on it, discipline and an understanding of why he's doing what he is are necessary. In principle, the correct attitude towards the discipline and practice of the Path of Self-Knowledge, in the beginning, is more important than the choice of the method. Regardless of whether he practices Vedanta or Yoga, Zen Buddhist meditation or Christian contemplation, it is essential that the seeker conduct his selected practice with understanding and that, from experience, he derive the principles that are the support of his practice.

Of course, the choice of method will ultimately depend on his psychophysical constitution. That is why the seeker must first get to know himself in order to choose the right method. Only then is he mature enough to comprehend the Path, which freely extends beyond all doctrines.

The following dominates in the Path's initial phase:

(a) the *technical principles of discipline*, such as focusing attention and cultivating composure, as well as the arts of self-analysis and pure unmotivated observation.

In the Path's middle phase, the following takes precedence:

(b) the *psychological principles of discipline*: the will to maintain the composure and vigilance with which practice is conducted, openness to every phenomenon and blink of consciousness without attachment, rejection or selection.

Fundamental in the Path's higher phase is:

(c) the *spiritual principle of each discipline*, and that is devotion to every breath, every step or stroke, to every act that we live by and that makes us who we are, without the expectation that we will get anything in return.

He who has not developed such *dedication* is unlikely to persist in his efforts to return to the Source using the upstream path. But little by little, he who has persisted despite all the ego's resistance will reach the phase in which the seeker intuitively grasps the Path, and his consciousness spontaneously balances itself out in its center.

III.6 The undivided self-identity of consciousness that is freed of relations

The deeper we penetrate into the reality behind the veil, the more we realize that the space through which we are moving is our consciousness's space and that whatever it is that we confront in that space, we are actually confronting ourselves; and whatever we accept in that space, with it we accept the unawakened aspects of our own being.

Being "*I*" or residing in the state of "*I am*" does not mean being an ideal, static persona, assimilated from the past (*how I was*) and projected into the future (*how I would like to be*). Being "*I*" means to be, through all the changes and transformations of the dynamics of personal self-development, to be aware of the *fundamental "I" here/now* like the spiritual core around which individual existence revolves like a vortex around its invisible, or better yet, *empty center.*

Until man accepts himself as he is, being aware that in the evolutionary running start he is different at every moment, he will not be able to accept others, or the world or reality as they are. Hidden in this rejection is the deeply buried fear of separation between *the I and the other*, and the primal pain of the first split between *the ego and the Self*, as the mental negative of all subsequent human divides.

Through personal growth, accepting ourselves with all our changes, little by little we start to accept reality as the dynamic expression of the absolute Self which expresses and makes itself self-aware complementarily through each individual being and creation as a whole, in a way that is incomprehensible to the individual that hasn't fully penetrated the veil of individual existence.

However, the deeper we penetrate into the reality behind the veil, the more we realize that the space through which we are moving is our *consciousness's* space and that whatever it is that we confront in that space, we are actually confronting ourselves; and whatever we accept in that space, with it we accept the unawakened aspects of our own being. Finally, the unreserved acceptance and integration of various aspects of existence leads to the expansion of consciousness to its undivided self-identity with the absolute Self.

For all that we accept and integrate represents the transformation of mental energy from our psyche's unawakened to its conscious field. Until ultimately all that remains is that which we primordially are and cannot not be – absolute undifferentiated *consciousness per se*, withdrawn from the antagonistic relationship between *self-awareness* as opposed to *awareness of the world of objects*, freed of all relations in its own *self-identity*.

III.7 *Who am I* or the traveler in search of his *authenticity*

(The Buddhist and Vedantist Path with Neuropsychological commentary)

Some call this transition from supported consciousness to continuous awakenness – Enlightenment, and others call it a quiet return to our Original Nature which we had never really lost. Having got enmeshed in our imagination and dreams, we had just briefly forgotten it.

No matter how much we listen, read or think about it, no voyage can truly begin until the traveler takes his first step onto the Path. All great spiritual traditions speak of this paradox, of the loom, the tension that prevails between the Path and the passenger, like that between the lyre and the bow.

From ancient Greek sages like Heraclitus and Socrates who said that *knowledge of the self* is ultimate purpose and meaning of philosophy (Heraclitus said: "All men have a share in self-knowledge and sound thinking") to Jesus's messages *in the Gnostic gospels*, such as the following one: "He who knows the all, but fails to know himself, misses everything"; to the founder of Buddhism, Gautama Buddha who teaches his first students these simple and direct words: "Be a light unto yourself!", to the to modern Vedanta teacher Ramana Maharshi who teaches that all the teachings of the Vedas and Upanishads can be reduced to a single question: "Who am I?".

However, the answer to this question, when it is not the result of a final spiritual attainment or self-realization, is conditioned by the level of understanding and identification with that *I* in various spiritual traditions. Almost all traditions distinguish the unconditional or *true I* from the conditioned or *illusory ego*.

Here we will not deal with the characteristics, similarities and differences of the many different Eastern and Western psychologies, because a serious comparison would require a separate study. Therefore, we will take this opportunity to focus on only two psychological models that demonstrate how the *illusory ego* is formed as the central cause of all our mistakes and problems, and how we can free ourselves from it.

Here in brief are the teachings of the *Vijnanavada* school of Mahayana Buddhism (in which *only Consciousness* is real and all other phenomena are but its modes) whose psychological-meditative model was chosen and exposed in a simplified way here because of its clarity, directness and practicality.

All our impressions (*samskaras*) that we have accumulated over a number of (re)incarnations, and based on them developed personal preferences and desires (*vasanas*) are in a latent state in the so-called treasury of consciousness (*Alaya-Vijnana*). It is important here to note that the Vijnanavada School distinguished between the *relative alaya* (synonymous to *chitta* in Vedanta psychology) which is still interdependent on all stored impressions, and *absolute alaya* (the equivalent of chit in Vedanta psychology) which is a spotless, self-illuminating *pure Consciousness* that is beyond all phenomena and karmic seeds. Paramartha, the Buddhist teacher from the 6th century who translated the Vijnanavada School's main texts into Chinese, called this basic unconditioned consciousness *amala vijnana* and explains it as being identical to our original, transpersonal – or Buddha-nature, which is common to all beings. (According to later interpretations *alaya* can be understood as the active and dynamic aspect whereas *amala* is the passive and static aspect of the one and same *basic consciousness* which is the basis of all manifested phenomena.)

So, in *alaya* all beings and phenomena unconsciously participate. They emerge out of alaya, through karmic conditions and causes like waves from an ocean, briefly giving the illusion of individual existence, and then their existence again dissolves into its primordial, impersonal nature. When karmic circumstances and causes (the universal network of cause and effect which affects all phenomena and all beings and occurs simultaneously with the manifestation of creation) encourage the manifestation of accumulated impressions and preferences, they rise from *alaya* in the area of individual, sensory awareness (*mano-vijnana*). But there they cannot come in a clean, unprocessed form because they pass through the filter of discriminatory mind (*manas*) which is like a membrane between the treasury of consciousness and consciousness's senses.

Before these mental impulses reach consciousness, our discriminative mind censors them like some sort of *Grand Inquisitor*, giving them attributes (form and name) according to its inherent and educational conditionnedness. Thus, unconscious impressions and preferences, while they cross the path from being unconscious to being conscious, transform from being a clean, neutral energy to being established desires, feelings, thoughts, images, etc.

There is no other way for that *primordial energy* to reach consciousness without personal interpretation, except *simply* through a nonadhesive *consciousness*. With such a *consciousness* (which could be succinctly described as a nonadhesive *neutral presence*) we stop the automatic rotation of the discriminatory center, which with its constant rotating (like the wheel in a well) lifts some impression from the bottom of the unconscious to an area of consciousness, and stores and lowers the others (which it receives through the five senses and the sensory mind) in the bottom of that same well or treasury of consciousness.

This is how alaya, with its constant boiling, manas with its discrimination, and mano-vijnana with its self-capturing for impressions, experiences and desires, crucify and turn us on *samsara's* wheel.

The most direct way to reach the freedom of Awakening is by maintaining a nonadhesive consciousness which stops the discriminating mind and the imaginary divide between collective and individual consciousness, and after long and persistent practice suddenly awakens us into the primordial undivided Consciousness as our unconditioned True Nature.

Some call this transition from supported consciousness to continuous awakenness – Enlightenment, and others call it a quiet return to our True Nature which we had never really lost. Having got enmeshed in our imagination and dreams, we had just briefly forgotten it. (And though that *"briefly"* in practice may represent dozens of lives and incarnations, this means nothing to the awakened, for True Nature knows no categories of space and time.)

As we have seen here, a focus on the *basis* is characteristic of Eastern psychologies (for Buddhists the *fundamental or authentic consciousness*, for Vedantists *the Self*) which on the personal plan is simultaneously seen as the center and the whole of our consciousness. Meanwhile Western psychology is primarily concerned with the central conscious pole of our psychic structure or ego. While Western psychology considers the ego to be the center of the conscious organization of individuality, Eastern psychology considers the ego (ahamkara) or the self-conscious discriminatory center (manas) to be the center of the divide between the *I* and the *other*, between the inner and the outer, low and sublime, pure and impure, etc.

Consequently, Eastern psychologies, Buddhist and Vedantist for example, claim this would-be (temporary or transitional) *ego-center* is the key cause of our internal divides, as well as the conflicts and neuroses that result from them. All of Eastern psychology's efforts, regardless of the number and variety of methods, ultimately boil down to finding a way to decompose this *imaginary* egocentric mental self, built from unconscious impressions, preferences and ideas about the *ego*, to take away its power over the life of the individual in order to reveal the authentic core of our Being or Self.

The shortest and most direct way to Self-actualization was briefly outlined in the teachings of the famous teacher of *Vedanta*, Ramana Maharshi. Simply, practically and in a way that wasn't inclined to intellectual theorizing, Sri Ramana explained the functioning of the human psyche to his disciples, comparing it to the projection of a film in a theater. The repository of our impressions (chitta) is coiled like a filmstrip. The mind (manas) is like the cinema projector through which the stored content of our memory is projected on the canvas of our authentic or unconditioned Consciousness (chit). And our illusory or conditioned *ego* (ahamkara) is the spectator who sits in the cinema and identifies with the film he is watching on the screen, forgetting that everything that he sees actually a projection of the content stored in the unconscious pole of his psyche.

If we accept this interpretation as credible, the following question is inevitably raised: How then can we wake from the self-forgetfulness of identification with the illusory and awaken our True Self? This is where the so-called higher, purified mind or *buddhi* jumps in (translated from Sanskrit into English *buddhi* is usually translated as *intellect*, although this is not the best translation) which has the ability, through analogy, to understand this "fallacy" and awaken our True Self through self-inquiry and self-reflection.

In Sanskrit Ramana calls this introspection *vichara*, and it is carried out in such a fashion that the practitioner answers to all affective and adhering manifestations of mind (selfish instincts, feelings, thoughts and desires) with the following counter--claims: "Who are these selfish desires coming to? Where are these egocentric thoughts coming from? Who is clutching to these self-centered feelings?" As the answer to all these questions points to the selfish center of our pseudo-identity or *false ego*, the culmination of this practice boils down to the question: "Who am I?" which is persistently repeated until the Awakening (*turiya*) of our True Being brings us liberation and puts an end to all of the mind's illusory questions.

But despite its simplicity, *vichara* is a superior contemplative practice that requires a subtly attentive mind and a sharp intellect in order for it to be properly applied. For lack of a better explanation, let his quote from the teachings of the Ramana Maharshi speak of its directness and efficiency: "Questioning '*Who am I?*' within one's mind, when one reaches the Heart, the individual '*I*' sinks crestfallen, and at once Reality manifests itself as 'I-I'. Though it reveals itself thus, it is not the egocentric '*I*' but the perfect being, the Self Absolute."

Interestingly, something similar can be found in the practical lessons of early Christian desert fathers whose contemplative teachings could be reduced to three fundamental principles: "Do not judge anything or anyone! Ask yourself who you are! Surrender everything to God!" But in this case, self-inquiry and Christian contemplative prayer are mutually supported and the result of this practice completely surrenders itself to God's will.

Well, let us look how modern neuropsychology interpret the complex phenomenon of human perception. From a scientific perspective, every perception requires three basic elements:

    a. sensory stimulus (sound, visual, tactile, etc.),

    b. sensory organ that receives a specific stimulus (ear, eye, skin),

    c. neural circuit in the brain, that senses receive sensory signals from, and organizes them in a determined way, giving them a specific interpretation and meaning.

When the eye perceives a particular subject, it does not recognize it immediately. First the optic nerves – sensory neurons which exist in the eye – detect a specific object in the space. Encouraged by this stimulus, neurons begin to bombard the thalamus, neuronal structure located in the center of the brain, with messages. The thalamus functions as a control panel with switches. It collects and classifies sensory messages, before they are transferred to the other parts of the brain.

In the case of visual perception, when the thalamus has sorted the messages sent by the optic nerves, they are transferred to the limbic system – the part of the brain responsible for processing emotional responses to sensory stimuli, in the form of pleasure or discomfort. At this stage of processing, the human brain brings immediate judgment on the respective visual stimulus, and decide whether the observed object is: pleasant, unpleasant or neutral.

While the limbic brain processes the received data, they are simultaneously transferred to the neocortex – the youngest part of the human brain, which is responsible for the analytical operations. The group of data, collected by the thalamus and partially processed by the limbic system, in neocortex forms a kind of analytical matrix through which our brain recognizes the perceived object, giving it a standard name and its meaning. Only by virtue of this, the existing matrix, our brain can distinguish, in a split second, a rope from a snake, and bring instanteneous, fateful decision. But this is possible only if the neocortex have already created a wide network of experiential patterns or, to put it simply, a map that helps us to position ourselves in the dynamic world of, only conditionally and not geometrically determined, approximations.

In other words, this summarized neuropsychological model of perception clearly shows us, that we can not directly experience this world, and that this experience is filtered through a layered and dynamic matrix of perception, which is constantly created and recreated by our brain, with all its – sensory, emotional and analytical, conceptual functions. What is the reality – you will rightfully ask – the objective world that we see, or our subjective world of experience and interpretation? The real answer would be: Neither world of objects, nor our subjective world, but a world in which the distinction between object and subject of perception has been transcended. Or, more precisely, the reality in which the perception of the object is not different from the mind which observes the object. But it is an experience that by far surpasses the area of the certainty of the scientific experiment and proof. The experience which directly can testify only – the Awakened.

Having said this, we can easily understand that the Path to Self-Knowledge is long and winding, and that its success, like a sage's tripod, lies in the balance of three strong-points:

    a. the ability to proper understand teachings (doctrines),
    b. the ability to properly select and in a balanced manner apply practical disciplines (methods),
    c. and finally, the most important thing without which all doctrines and methods are unable to bring the much desired fruit: a deep personal dedication to our original Being (devotion), in which, in the end, we recognize our*selves*, our teacher and God as the one indivisible True Self.

But all these are only *signs along the Path* that, the deeper we dive into them, the clearer they alert us that we cannot really know anything about the Path until we travel it.

IV. THE AWAKENED MAN: THE HERETIC, THE ANARCHIST, THE REBEL

To become free, to be liberated from slavery: this is what a man ought to strive for when he becomes even a little conscious of his position. There is nothing else for him, and nothing else is possible so long as he remains a slave both inwardly and outwardly. But he cannot cease to be a slave outwardly while he remains a slave inwardly. Therefore in order to become free, man must gain inner freedom.

G. I. Gurdjieff

If you act as a reformer then you are patching up society, which is always degenerating, and so sustaining a system which has produced wars, divisions and separativeness. The reformer, really, is a danger to the fundamental change of man. You have to be an outsider to all communities, to all religions and to the morality of society, otherwise you will be caught in the some old pattern, perhaps somewhat modified.

Jiddu Krishnamurti: The Only Revolution

IV.1 The doors we went out through are the same ones we must come back through

Whenever we don't act with honesty, then we are not living from our heart. Whenever we try to deceive our heart, some-

thing in us resists and taking the roundabout, brings us back to the beginning of the path. For the doors we went out through are the same we must come back through.

A painful ambivalence will exist in man until he accepts pain as a part of life. Trying to protect himself from pain, trying to savor life in a *minimal risk space*, man inevitably raises walls around him, the walls of his own prison. Dividing himself from the uncertainties of life, he is separated from his *unknown self*, denying himself the opportunity to ever fully get to know himself. And such a life, as the prisoner of one's own *escape into freedom*, in exchange for the illusory security of the prison, is not really life; rather, it is giving up on life, a quiet starvation.

In spite of everything, it is precisely out of this unknown self that inexorably rises the endless yearning for freedom, the heart's or the soul's yearning to jump over the extortive mind's walls, a longing that doesn't allow you to give in to and perish as the slave of your own fear. And though for a long time man will continue to in the morning erect the walls that he jumps over in the evening, that yearning will not give him peace until the final dawn, outside all walls.

When we are not authentic, when we make compromises and fulfill external requirements out of pure commotion because accommodation seems easier and safer than confrontation, this is when avoided, unresolved conflicts will lead the internal struggle in us.

From the outside we will seem to accept, but from the inside, though it be unconsciously, we will sabotage, reject, ignore... Whenever we do not honestly tackle specific life challenges, we betray ourselves on the inside and cannot easily forgive ourselves, nor can we forgive whoever has set us the challenge. That is why authenticity is a prerequisite for an honest and clear relationship, both with ourselves and with other human beings, on all levels.

Whenever we don't act with honesty, then we are not living from our *heart*. Whenever we try to deceive our heart, something in us resists and taking the roundabout, brings us back to the beginning of the path. For the doors we went out through are the same we must come back through.

IV.2 How can we step out of the psychological trap called the double-bind?

There is no magic here. It is simply a psychological trap called double bind, which is tightened by any attempt of control, and can only be loosened by an acceptance of circumstances and a release of attachment. In theory this sounds simple but in practice it cannot be properly understood until we get out of it, nor can we get out of it until we resolve it from within.

Ceasing to bind oneself to egocentric desires, feelings and thoughts, where *ego-saprophyte* becomes parasite, is not possible by willingly distancing ourselves from them. Because the mere act of willing, which does not come from the conscious center (or spiritual heart), sets off the ego's controlling activities, and hence its empowerment.

That is why we must cut the root of selfish desires, feelings and thoughts, and this is the root of *selfish motivation* that comes from the ego's instinctive need to control its circumstances and self-preservation, drawing the being's intense energy in order to fortify its fortress's walls.

This motivation is actually quite simple: *I-mine-for me*. And it constantly produces the desires, feelings and thoughts that feed and develop it. It is only when man learns, in a single impulse of the mind, to recognize this selfish motivation and to *release* it right away, not clutching to it, that the *ego's root* will gradually dry up and its branches (selfish desires, feelings, thoughts, actions) will fall off by themselves.

For *release* (as opposed to adhesion which leads to attachment to and rising of inner walls) is a spontaneous act of the heart or of the center of consciousness, while control through the repression and rationalization of the same impulses (not because we have personally identified them as inappropriate but because society and culture condemned them as being unsuitable) is a violent act of the ego.

Through self-deceiving control, the ego is not abolished but rather artificially corrected, coming across as being even more tenacious and treacherous behind the thicker and more impenetrable layers of the socio-cultural mask or *persona*. Such an ego is like a tough weed against which man can fight hard all his life, without ever succeeding in plucking it out.

Until basic selfish motivation is dried out (that foundation from which the ego grows like a saprophyte) whether it be through contemplative coming into awareness and conscious release or through karmically conditioned living conditions and relations, which is a much more difficult painful lesson, this *chameleon's* body will not be beheaded.

And this is the meaning behind Christ's simple messages about the need to forgive and forget debts on the path to liberation from the shackles that our inner judge bound us to; for if we do not forgive others, we will not be able to forgive ourselves. If we do not relieve debtors of their *debts*, we most certainly will rigidly continue to carry our own debts like a burden that we carry on our backs.

There is no *magic* here. It is simply a psychological trap called *double bind*, which is (aggressively-adherently or passive-ignorantly) tightened by any attempt of control, and can only be loosened by an acceptance of circumstances and a release of attachment. In theory this sounds simple but in practice it cannot be properly understood until we get out of it, nor can we get out of it until we resolve it from within.

How then can we get out of the double bind? By accepting that understanding and liberation, insight and stepping out of the trap, all happen simultaneously.

IV.3 The path to presence – sailing the unstable winds of change

The body only spontaneously acts as a whole when a discriminatory mind (manas) which constantly divides and judges both our external and our internal worlds into good and bad, desirable and repulsive is for a while calmed, muted, absent. That is when the body is harmoniously saturated, initiated and led by an unimpeded stream of consciousness/energy.

On the path to presence, the body has three main advantages over the mind. First, the body is always present, while the mind is usually absent. Second, the body naturally functions as a whole, while the mind is composed of a series of functions (memory, reasoning, attention, will, etc.) and groupings of impressions (samskaras) which often trigger the mind to work in incompatible and conflicting directions.

For example, one group of samskaras can motivate you to devote yourself to your studies and to science. But at the same time another group of samskaras is pulling you towards quitting your studies and completely devoting yourself to artistic research and creation. In our unconscious, there are many groups of samskaras, accumulated over a number of incarnations, which under certain conditions and when caused by specific circumstances, rise to consciousness's surface and seek to actualize themselves into reality. A focused and calm mind is required to determine priorities and to avoid the internal conflicts of discordant and rival groups of samskaras.

Third, the body only spontaneously acts as a whole when a discriminatory mind (manas), which constantly divides and judges both our external and our internal worlds into good and bad, desirable and repulsive, is for a while calmed, muted, absent. That is when the body is harmoniously saturated, initiated and led by an unimpeded stream of consciousness/energy.

This absence of manas and of the unobstructed flow of our original consciousness/energy is difficult to achieve and even more difficult to maintain without regular meditation; whether it be the seated meditation that is practiced in yoga and Zen Buddhism or moving meditation such as tai chi chuan, chi kung and other kinds of Taoist exercises. However, despite the mentioned advantages, exercises in which the body dominates will not produce the desired results if they do not maximally include awareness, or simply presence; for the body without an engaged consciousness acts instinctively, inertly, automatically and hence unconsciously.

Therefore the path to presence is best explained as being the body (whether in motion or at rest) plus consciousness. And this simple path does not require any other interventions from our behalf except: awaken it and become it!

Then there is no need for the self-aware discriminatory mind, which wants to keep everything around it under control, to return from its absence, just like the fog does not need to fill in the valley when the light of dawn is shone on it.

However, the nature of change (as the basic principle that governs the universe) does not allow any state to be permanently maintained. The mind will reappear like the shadow follows the form, like fog follows heavy clouds. But he who has discovered the power of presence will never let himself be deceived by the illusion of change again; he will simply remain present and wait for the wheels of change to turn, for the clouds to disperse, for the fog to lift, for the sun to shine behind the shroud of deception.

On this path, no longer can anything be done except to stay awake, lucid and to navigate from moment to moment, from wave to wave, to sail aligning oneself to the unstable winds of change.

IV.4 All that we can become is nothing compared to that which we truly are

That which we present ourselves to be shows not what we are, rather it hides that which we think we are. That which we think we are has nothing to do with what we actually are. We can only awaken what we truly are when we break all ties with that which we present ourselves to be and with that which we think we are.

When a man gives up his authenticity in exchange for social acceptance and confirmation, that is when the Self's blossoming stops, and this great psychological divide between what we really are and what we strive to become (in order to be accepted) tries to create a bridge made of insatiable ambition.

However, you can become a doctor of science, or Olympic champion and Nobel Prize winner, anything, but this will not and cannot fulfill the insatiable emptiness that is expanding in you until you see the tragicomic paradox that has been playing with you the whole time: that all that you can become is nothing compared to that which you already are.

Waking up, blossoming, making actual and present that which we are in our lives is the only calling that existence gives us. All the other callings are put before us by society. It is up to us to choose whether we will follow society's or life's callings and criteria. It is our life; it cannot be sold or bargained for.

Luckily there is no compensation that can fill the spiritual void in the man who sincerely seeks that which is inalienable, which is most proper in oneself. Just like Jesus said: "Woe to you who have received your consolation on earth". When we understand this we begin to go back to the path of the return to our authenticity. And there begins the path of the healing and cleansing of the false and the awakening of the authentic.

Although there is nothing more certain in human existence than the fact that *I am*, there is no *certainty* in this complex existence called *man* that is more often questioned and more difficult to accept.

On the other hand, no matter how much some teachings try to prove that there is no *stable ego* which could confirm itself (with words, actions or *simply by being silent*) with the unconditional and lasting affirmation *I Am*, should we examine this type of teaching's consequences (contemplatively and not just intellectually) we will find that the *ego* that denies the existence of an *I* is no different from the senile old man who, when hearing the ring of trick-or-treaters at the door, simply answers that *there's no one at home.*

Indeed, this *self-negating ego* is so attached to itself that at all costs it tries to preserve itself using intellectual detours: *"You see, no "Ego" exists, so we don't have to free ourselves from it!"*

But what each real *Path to Self-Knowledge* calls us to is the need to awaken the indestructible existence of the true, *unborn I* in order for this *false ego*, which resiliently affirms itself through self-denial, to disappear without a trace in the end.

This *false ego's* entire self-preservation strategy boils down to three steps which constantly intertwine and trip over themselves and which in short can be expressed in three maxims:

1. That which we present ourselves to be shows not what we are, rather it hides that which we think we are.

2. That which we think we are has nothing to do with what we actually are.

3. We can only awaken what we truly are when we break all ties with that which we present ourselves to be and with that which we think we are.

It is not necessary to point out that the only way out of this vicious circle is through *Awakening*.

IV.5 The Awakened Man: the Heretic, the Anarchist, the Rebel

He is a Heretic for religions that have been deceiving the naive for millennia, he is a Anarchist for political ideologies that have been exploiting the small-minded since ancient times, he is a Rebel for the pseudo-culture which only entertains and lulls the deluded masses to sleep in the false belief that our culture outlives us, and thus gives meaning to the barren, bovine senselessness of unconscious human existence.

Fear comes from the lust to live, and lust comes from the misconception that we are an individual that is separate from the Wholeness of life. The notion of the *divided ego* isolates us in the cocoon of egoism and separates us from the universal source of life energy/consciousness. This cocoon creates a divide between the *ego* and the Wholeness, a deep divide, as immeasurable as the abyss and endlessly empty, empty...

We try to fill this lifeless emptiness, this dead marsh with false relationships and with dead objects. Life may pass us by in our attempt to fulfill it, but we will not succeed until we get out of the egocentric cocoon and make contact with the universal source of consciousness/energy.

However, man cannot do so until he grasps how illusory the idea of a *divided ego* is. Man is supported in this illusion by a society, culture and civilization built on the religious and ideological manipulation, political subjugation and economic exploitation of the deceived and narrow-minded masses.

Let's face it: society and political, ideological or religious organizations, or any kind of *interest group* for that matter, has no use of the individual that has come out of his mental cocoon and returned to the Source of his being. Furthermore, the liberated individual does not need such a community that is based on common interest and rough trade. Only the ego needs the community to ratify it, because the ego with no relationships and relations is *nothing*, no matter how calculated and hypocritical these relationships be.

On the other hand, only the ego that supports the said mental divide needs that quasi-cultural cheap jewelry, all that manipulative human vanity and sensory-teasing reservoir to at least seemingly keep it alive, to conceal from it the bitter truth that is has been dead, unreal in fact, from the very beginning.

The man who has left the ego's cocoon and returned to the source of energy/consciousness is like a cup that overflows with life and consciousness. For him, the divide and the emptiness that needs to be filled no longer exist, he no longer needs the toys and rattles that society produces for the infantile, for him the community's confirmation or odium no longer mean a thing, and in this respect, he is beyond the reach of any manipulation.

Since he has awakened the indivisible unity of life within himself, and the knowledge that this is also reflected in every being (to the extent of and according to its level of development), it is clear to him that all relationships and relations are but the One's game, or to be more exact, that this whole world is the theatre in which It is the writer, director and actor.

Were many able to grasp this, theatres and operas could be free to close their doors, film companies could be turned into funeral homes, the entertainment, museum and gallery industries, without feeling any remorse, could become utility services, and forests would no longer need to be cut down for the production of trivial *trash novels*, which today are haughtily christened *literature*.

This superficial, cursory, Potemkin culture, or better said, artificial decoration, that supports and manipulates a false picture of the world and of man, becomes more worthless than discarded packaging for the one who can see through the spider web that man has been feeding off, wrapping himself in, deceiving himself with since the beginning of mankind. It is tragicomic but true that such a *liberated individual* is not needed by anyone, because ultimately he is fulfilled by himself and is beyond all relations, undivided like the original One.

He is a *Heretic* for religions that have been deceiving the naive for millennia, he is a *Anarchist* for political ideologies that have been exploiting the small-minded since ancient times, he is a *Rebel* for the pseudo-culture which only entertains and lulls the deluded masses to sleep in the false belief that our culture outlives us, thus giving meaning to the barren, bovine senselessness of unconscious human existence.

Finally, what is probably the most painful for the *global marketplace* which is represented by the *civilization of Homo Sapiens* is that you cannot do business with the Awakened Man. He has nothing to offer because he knows that his inexhaustible personal treasury is available to every man. You cannot sell him anything, because at every step he takes he finds this Garden of Eden's rich fruit, whose heirs are all those who have returned to themselves. He has nothing to share with anyone, because he has seen that we are all nevertheless immersed in that which is originally Indivisible, like fish in water.

What a joy it is to meet the liberated man on the Path and to continue to travel with him, in perfect silence, without a voice. Such a man has no other option but to travel without making any stops, to proceed while avoiding all dams, docks, coasts...

IV.6 The bridge to the other bank: where there is no distance between *being, knowing* and *doing*

In this self-developmental phase the unconsciously monolithic man becomes a split being that is delirious over the abyss of existence who has a huge question mark hanging over his head like a noose. Hamlet's eternal question for him is not "to be or not to be" but rather "to grab on or to let go".

It is only while he is active (and while there is no room for doubt) that man is whole and free of divides within himself.

Moreover, in the given act he is identical to himself, without the censorship, analysis and criticism that the egocentric mind includes in the *play* right before or after the act.

That which makes the blissfulness of the very act insufficient is the fact that while man is acting he has no time for observation and that is when much escapes him. That is why, every so often, it is necessary for him to go from acting to contemplation or observation in order to more clearly see himself and the world around him in the mirror of self-reflection.

However, the more reflective a man is, the more he sees the details and controversies that give birth to questions, doubt and inner conflicts within him... All this might make him more reasonable but also less apt for immediate and effective action. Moreover, the very process of self-reflection divides him, making him both the subject and object of consideration, stripping him of his primary *wholeness* and *self-identity*.

In this self-developmental phase the unconsciously monolithic man becomes a *split being* that is delirious over the abyss of existence who has a huge question mark hanging over his head like a noose. Hamlet's eternal question for him is not *"to be or not to be"* but rather *"to grab on or to let go"*.

At this developmental level, the human *I* acts like an electron in an atomic shell. When it is moving or acting, it is *self--identical* but it cannot clearly *self-determine* itself, because the I is always determined in relation to another or to something different from itself. When it is inactive a clear self-determination is possible, but such a state is much less effective in the existential-active sense.

Building on Heisenberg's *uncertainty principle* which states that the position and speed of atomic particles cannot precisely be simultaneously determined, we could characterize this state of consciousness as the impossibility of *consistent self-determination*.

In addition, in such a state of *passive self-reflection* man finds himself in the paradoxical absurdity of his existence, recognizing that he is *blind in his acting*, and *redundant in his inaction*, redundant in terms of his own position within the natural wholeness whose spontaneity is violated by self-inquiry.

Fortunately, this condition is transitory and is not the end of man's search for his own identity, meaning and authenticity. It is just a bridge to the other bank, the bridge from unconscious-instinctual existence towards conscious-volitional life. Derived from everything that we have gone through, the *other bank* should be man's rediscovered and reestablished unity with his Self and with nature as a whole.

So, how can we achieve that state of mind in which there no longer are any divides or distance in time between *being, knowing and doing*? The answer to this question is not a matter of philosophical discourse or of psychological analysis, but rather the practical Path to self-knowledge.

IV.7 He who searches finds nothing, until he loses the One who searches

When I searched for a witness, in whose conscience this game of hide and seek takes place and uncovers itself, the game just magically disappeared... And again I found nothing, and therefore lost the One who did the searching.

When I searched for the mind I could not find it. I only found thoughts and ideas, feelings, desires and instincts, the many mental impressions that had sprung up from the bottom of the unconscious like sediment that is surfaced by the constant rippling of consciousness. When I searched for the origin of the mind (its source and delta), I could not find it. I only found an open circle which is created in the unconscious desire for affirmation and is continued through actions that give rise to new desires.

When I searched for the ego that appropriates the products of the mind's activities, I could not find it. All I found was beginningless and infinite consciousness's flux that pulsates rhythmically, like the high tide raising the waves of mental impressions from its bottom and like the low tide bringing them back down to rest.

The I in this process was just a bystander who, misled by the waves' game, self-obliterated and got entwined in their game, identified with the castaway without a strong-point. But in reality I found no actor at all, just spontaneous actions that take place unprompted.

When I searched for a witness, in whose conscience this game of hide and seek takes place and uncovers itself, the game just magically disappeared... And again I found nothing, and therefore lost the One who did the searching.

> *In the end,*
> *the mirror had just magically*
> *mirrored itself, lit itself up...*

V. FREEDOM BEYOND MIND AND TIME

Like the Eastern void, the "physical vacuum" – as it is called in field theory – is not a state of mere nothingness, but contains the potentiality for all forms of the particle world. These forms, in turn, are not independent physical entities, but merely transient manifestations of the underlying nothingness. As the Mahayana Heart Sutra says, "Form is emptiness, and emptiness is indeed form."

Fritjof Capra: The Tao of Physics

When attention is strongly developed, awareness appears even from within our negativity, and from that awareness comes our meditation. We see that everything that occurs is a manifestation of energy, which itself is a form of our awareness, and we realize that all experience, each of the twenty-four hours of the day, is a part of the enlightenment nature.

Tarthang Tulku: Openness Mind

V.1 Identification and consciousness – the two sides of the dynamic *tapestry of the mind*

As soon as a thought arose on identity and on the relation between the I (the hunter) and the other (the prey), the unity of reality and consciousness was broken into a myriad of "living splinters" like a mirror. In this example, in the quiet savannah of consciousness, the hunter is just the mind which in a single shot of ambition scattered the savannah's quiet beauty into an immovable flow

Awareness is not identification. Awareness is the perception of the world as *suchness*, without the will and effort to identify and define it. For as soon as we identify and define a specific object, we have divided it from the Whole, we have divided the totality of reality and thus the integrity of our mind, because reality as a manifested world and the mind that perceives it are interdependent and inseparable, much like the two sides of a tapestry.

When we are aware all that we see is *just That!* When we identify, "That" becomes a set of attributes attached to "That" by our mind through the fives functions (*skandhas*) of the cognitive chain: form, sensation, perception, impressions and consciousness.

The Spiritual heart (*hridaya*) is the source from which the mind or the power of consciousness (*chitishakti*) runs, simultaneously reflects and illuminates the manifested world, and finally returns to the same source. When we are simply witnessing, the cognitive organon of the mind is not set in motion from our spiritual center; we perceive reality as a *dynamic tapestry* that is reflected in the calm mind like in a clean mirror with our undivided consciousness (*chit*). In such a contemplative awareness the reality that we experience and the consciousness that observes form an indivisible, dynamic whole.

As soon as the mind is set in motion from its center, it illuminates (*prakasha*) and identifies (*vimarsha*) the given object, and in doing so gives it attributes that are congruent with its major functions: perception registers it, impressions define our relationship (i. e. is the object attractive or repulsive to us), sensation determines the desire to appropriate or reject the object, the form of the object itself restricts it to a number of possible functions according to which we define its 'usability', and finally thought *names* it and classifies it under a particular conceptual category. With such a *functional* observation the mind divides the world into an observed object and an observing subject and it simultaneously divides itself and the wholeness of reality.

Therefore, we can only awaken the true identity of the *Self/Reality* through contemplative (mirroring but not reflective) consciousness, and not through functional identification, speculative definition and abstract concepts.

We will consider how this cognitive principle works in the following example. The hunter who lies quietly on his hunting stand in the middle of the savannah observing the environment maintains a vigilant, neutral awareness until his attention is captured by and focused on a single object. As soon as he tries to identify it, his stream of his consciousness, which was uninterrupted until then, is interrupted and his mind springs into action. The thought that identifies the object springs up (e. g. the antelope that quenches its thirst at a nearby source) and then pulls the chain of elements or the functions of the cognitive organon from consciousness's latent reservoir of contents (chitta). And so the specific thought pulls along the corresponding impressions (samskaras) that are stored in the memory, the impressions trigger the congruent desire (vasanas), e. g. "I want this antelope!" and the desire prompts an action (kriya) – the hunter shoots an arrow into the antelope.

And with this seemingly imperceptible gesture, with one tug of the bow's string the totality of the savannah's unity was shattered. Until that moment, the hunter, the antelope and the source formed the whole harmony of the quiet savannah. As soon as a thought arose on identity and on the relation between the *I* (the hunter) and the *other* (the prey), the unity of reality and consciousness was broken into a myriad of "living splinters" like a mirror. In this example, in the quiet savannah of consciousness, the hunter is just the mind which in a single shot of ambition scattered the savannah's quiet beauty into an immovable flow...

And what else is our existence but the elusive dance of countless 'living debris' which painfully screaming seek the focus through which they will return to the harmony of the lost Whole? And that focus we have jumped out of, thrown by inertia onto the periphery of our own rotation, is no other than the tunnel into the heart of our True Nature – undivided consciousness/reality.

V.2 Getting out of time means getting out of the *ego/mind*

The mind, space/time and motion are in fact identical, it is only subsequent abstracting and the analysis of direct experience and perception that divides them. Moreover, it is not even the analysis of experience but the analysis of the memory of an experience that is irretrievably gone.

The wind was flapping a temple flag, and two monks were arguing about the flag. One said, "The flag is moving." The other said, "the wind is moving." They could not agree, no matter how hard they debated. The sixth patriarch, Hui Neng, happened to come by and said, "Not the wind, not the flag. It is the mind that is moving!"

Mumonkan, case 29.

According to our personal experience in many years of studying the philosophy and practice of Zen Buddhism, this is one of the most important koans in Zen's thousands of years old tradition. It expresses the essence of the mind, of nature and of man, and its deep wisdom is confirmed by modern physics today.

Space and objects, motion and time appear with the mind and live only in the mind. Without the mind there is no space or objects, or motion or time. Did space come before motion and motion before time, or did time come before space and motion? These are redundant questions because all three occur simultaneously, and instantaneously disappear with the mind again.

Here's what the Korean modern Zen Master Seung Sahn (1927-2004) had to say about this, almost 1300 years after the greatest reformer of Chinese Zen, the famous sixth patriarch Hui Neng (638-713), but with the same original acuteness and sharpness of insight: *When all thinking has been cut off, you become empty mind. This is before thinking. Your "before thinking mind", my "before thinking mind", all people's "before thinking minds" are the same. This is your substance. Your substance, my substance, and the substance of the whole universe become one. So the tree, the mountain, the cloud and you become one."*

The mind, space/time and motion are in fact identical; it is only subsequent abstracting and the analysis of direct experience and perception that divides them. Moreover, it is not even the analysis of experience but the analysis of the *memory of an experience* that is irretrievably gone. When the mind is set in motion from its own center, its motion automatically includes space and time; therefore it is self-evident that these three are inseparable.

In his brilliant "The Mysterious Record of Immovable Wisdom," the lucid Japanese Zen master Takuan Soho (1573 to 1645) says: "The *No-Mind is the same as the Right Mind. It neither congeals nor fixes itself in one place. It is called No-Mind when the mind has neither discrimination nor thought but wanders about the entire body and extends throughout the entire self. (...) When this No-Mind has been well developed, the mind does not stop with one thing nor does it lack any one thing. It is like water overflowing and exists within itself. It appears appropriately when facing a time of need."*

Finally, when the mind goes back to the *center* (or its source) with it also goes back the entire manifested world of phenomena and states, for phenomena are nothing more than the changing forms of the dynamic nature of the mind's volatile states. But where is it going back? To your "before thinking mind" as Seung Sahn calls it or to the "No-Mind" as Hui Neng calls it. To the state before manifestation or before thinking, according to the Greek sage Heraclitus. "*Heraclitus says that the world was not created according to time, but to thought*"

(Aetius II 4,3). And all these different names point to one center, to the origin of all states and knowledge.

However, man cannot emerge from time until he identifies himself with the *individual ego*. It is only when he reveals his true, transpersonal Self (in Zen teachings this which is *authentic* to all beings is called *Buddha Nature*) that he will realize that it always and invariably is, beyond space and time.

Because the Self is neither born nor does it die. It is Unborn as is our steady identity, as said by Japanese Zen master Bankei Yotaku (1622 – 1693) in his unorthodox teachings: *"If you have the least desire to be better than you actually are, if you hurry up to the slightest degree in search of something, you are already going against the Unborn"*.

It is therefore the *authenticity* which we cannot reach or deny, simply because it is what we truly and inalienably *Are*, it is not created nor can it be ruined, (*"It shoots, It hits,"* renowned kyudo master Awa Kenzo would say) it does not move yet it is omnipresent, because everything that occurs changes and disappears, it moves about this absolute Self just like a fish in the infinite ocean.

V.3 Reality is pure consciousness/energy

This is the beginning of self-delusion: the replacement of phenomenon with nomen, fleeting phenomena with a permanent term, a being for a name, the replacement of a thread in the infinite and dynamic cosmic weave with the separate tapestry of thought which we will triumphantly expose in the imaginary gallery of exhibits and which in reality do not exist anywhere except in our minds.

In the entire infinite universe, only consciousness/energy is real and steady. Furthermore, to be more precise, the entire infinite universe is nothing more than consciousness/energy.

All of existence's phenomena are flighty, transient, changeable, and in their essence exist without their own, individual basis. These phenomena are really nothing more than that universal consciousness/energy's game. The same is true for the human body and the many aspects or functions of human consciousness (memory, feeling, thinking, will, observation...) which, for lack of a better definition, we group under the umbrella term mind.

Through this naming, defining, categorizing we classify a *transient phenomenon* in the register of thought concepts (*nomen*) and we give it an apparent detachment from the whole of reality, we give it individuality with all its attributes and seeming permanence.

This is the beginning of self-delusion: the replacement of *phenomenon with nomen*, fleeting phenomena with a permanent term, a being for a name, the replacement of a thread in the infinite and dynamic cosmic weave with the separate tapestry of thought which we will triumphantly expose in the imaginary gallery of exhibits and which in reality do not exist anywhere except in our *minds*.

By giving transient phenomena an apparent conceptual permanence, man unconsciously believes that he is ensuring that same permanence for himself, in this or another world, in this or another form of existence. But if we were to try to see each individual phenomena *as it really is* (in the moment of transience and change) without assigning it a name and the associated attributes, we might succeed in experiencing it in its essence: as dynamic consciousness/energy which constantly, continually moves, creates, scatters, in short plays by creating, reshaping, dissolving this world of dreams.

V.4 Insight into the True Nature is nothing but its *self-mirroring*

This delusion is an abyssal split in our being between self-delusion and authenticity. It is an abyss which cannot be filled with any kind of compensation, whether economic or with one's status, yet it is impossible to skip or circumvent because it is it is illusory, and therefore so is the jumper who is trying to skirt it.

Insight into the True Nature, what is that? Who has insight into what? And who is liberated by such insight? True Nature is always complete, undivided and omnipresent in every moment, in every unmeasurably short flash, of our own self-reflection. Who then would be able to see through it or achieve it? The false, *misguided ego* is not able to do so, and *seeing/achieving* is not necessary for the True I because It only knows, possesses self-reflects itself.

From this it can be said that True Nature – one, undivided, omnipresent and unchanging – *is unachievable and unknowable in Itself.* Any attempt to reach insight or achievement continues to feed the illusion about the path to self-realization. And all suffering is a result of this delusion, this idea that we exist divided from True Nature. And every attempt to overcome this delusion only further confirms it because it feeds it with its motivational energy.

And so the delusion about the ego, slavery and the path to liberation is the subtlest delusion, and it arises from initial ignorance. This delusion is an abyssal split in our being between self-delusion and authenticity. It is an abyss which cannot be filled with any kind of compensation, whether economic or with one's status, yet it is impossible to skip or circumvent because it is it is illusory, and therefore so is the jumper who is trying to skirt it.

What then can the man who finds himself on the brink of the abyss do, who with one wrong move can crash into nothingness? We can only find out when we abandon every ambition, expectation, relationship, because then all the bridges, which are really false relations, between the *ego* and the illusory world (which, like a spider web we have woven with the endless, self-recycling concepts of the mind) fall into nothingness, like the fog dissolves before the coming of dawn.

Does life confirm Nietzsche's famous dictum "Whoever fights monsters should see to it that in the process he does not become a monster. And if you gaze long enough into an abyss, the abyss will gaze back into you"? We maintain (believe, with more optimism than Nietzsche) that the man that hangs over the abyss and trembling looks into the nothingness that silently looks back at him, will not fall into the abyss if, even for a moment, he remembers *Who he Is*.

When we recall the True Self, we realize that That which remains after the dissolution of the delusion was always there. We had never even lost it, we never strayed, we were never chained... We were only, sometimes sweetly, sometimes bitterly, dreaming.

"That which remains, *but what is That?*" you will rightfully ask. That is always One thing, but to each seeker it is reflected anew as something else.

Never mind! But still...

> *In ten thousand sources*
> *ten thousand reflections,*
> *but only one Moon reflects itself.*

V.5 Where does the *cloud of ignorance* disappear to when it is no longer supported by our attention?

If we were only to ask ourselves what remains of that limited ego-consciousness when we stop archiving mental impressions, differentiating them, conceptualizing and identifying ourselves with our virtual concepts, we could see that this egocentric consciousness disappears like the dark cloud of ignorance when the energy of attention that had condensed it until then is withdrawn from it.

Where does this division of unique Consciousness into the conscious, subconscious, unconscious (let us add super-conscious) come from? Or division into memory, reason, intellect and ego...? All terms are relative because they are valid within specific philosophical systems and psychological teachings. They are less important because they are in principle only an aid and a support to practice.

However, the divides in our minds are evident in the same way that the states of being awake, of imagination and dreaming are. The existence of dreamless deep sleep is also known to us, although we do not *perceive* it through personal experience; but it is science that confirms it experimentally.

How can we explain the origin of the internal dynamics of consciousness and its transformation into different states? If we leave aside theories and concepts and impartially consider where all these divides come from, we will find that the following coexists in our psychic organization (on a broad scale ranging from complementarity to conflict): *That which is divided and He who divides*. Moreover, we will clearly see that *He who divides and That which he divides* are the true and indivisible Unity, we will see we ourselves are That.

This is where all internal conflicts come from, because there is an attempt to divide that which is itself indivisible, for the sake of control. And that which is indivisible, *You Are That!*, as confirms the ancient upanishadic saying *Tat Tvam Asi!* And that is why it is natural for your center, your *personal core* to spontaneously resist the counter-natural strategy of divide and control that our ego has unconsciously assimilated from its social and cultural environment.

This kind of *control strategy* proves itself to be tragicomically absurd if we realize that the very attempt to divide our own mental whole into the more valuable *controlling part* and into the less valuable *controlled part* implies a division within us. Where does this divide in the *originally undivided* come from, who or what encourages it and sets in motion?

Consciousness per se cannot divide, nor is it divisible. However, when the *Consciousness that is* is manifested in individuums, the identification of the individual's limited awareness along with the different functions of that authentic Consciousness appear. This is when the modifications in the authentic Consciousness in individuums are recognized and classified as separate functions: storing impressions or memory (chitta), differentiating and categorizing impressions (manas), creating conceptions (buddhi), identifying with concepts such as the *concept of the ego* (ahamkara)...

In doing so individualized limited consciousness forgets its *authentic identity* and, identifying itself with its limited functions, postulates *itself* as the only existing *ego-consciousness*. This is how the first delusions and divides within our authentic unique spiritual nature come to be.

But if we enter deeper into the process of self-awareness we might get to the level, or depth if you will, at which we will see that this mental divide is not real, that it is in fact like a dream that lasts while the "dreamer" (limited *ego-consciousness*) supports it with its identification to dreamt scenarios.

If we were only to ask ourselves what remains of that limited *ego-consciousness* when we stop archiving mental impressions, differentiating them, conceptualizing and identify ourselves with our *virtual concepts*, and if this wondering were to grow into a really deep nonadhesive observation, we could see that this *egocentric consciousness* disappears like the dark cloud of ignorance when the energy of attention that had condensed it until then is withdrawn from it.

What remains after that? This cannot be understood or described by the mind that is based on illusory divides and that consequently is itself an illusion. However, this could be experienced (and lived) by our entire Being once it awakens, recognizes and actualizes its true and indivisible spiritual unity.

V.6 The tragicomedy of the *walking paradox*: the duel between Consciousness and will

The tragicomedy of the walking paradox called man is that there is no obstacle that he cannot overcome, under the condition that he gives up the ambition that welcomes every new running start of his by raising the bar. If this paradox were completely seen through, is there anyone who would continue to languish like the prisoner of an invisible prison?

Will is the creative force with which Consciousness creates this endless world of countless phenomena. There is no beginning or end to creation. This supposed process or series of interrelated processes is in fact one endless flow of will that arises from Consciousness and returns to it.

In this flow, will transfigures itself into an innumerable multitude of beings through which Consciousness manifests itself. Therefore, that omnipresent Consciousness is the very essence of every being, and the will that moves in an eternal circle of efflux and sinking is its active side.

The will's unstoppable, all-penetrating circulation creates a *metaphysical labyrinth* within each being, creating in it the illusion of a seemingly autonomous ego and a mind separated from universal will. However, whoever penetrated into the center of the labyrinth through contemplation has seen that the mind and the ego are the two faces of one coin, two poles of a circle whose center is empty. How then did this mystery come to be?

When will is stirred within a being (and movement is in its nature), from the unconscious, it rises to the surface of consciousness the impressions that determine our preferences, either to the objective world of phenomena or to the subjective world of experience. According to these preferences, the individual being's limited universal will clutches to phenomena and experiences, and according to affinities, it feels attracted to or repulsed by them.

Since the exchange between attraction and repulsion constantly draws beings into the circle of death and birth it then experiences the pain that causes it to search for the basic root, in order to finally be freed from suffering and the cycle of successive incarnations.

In this quest for freedom, the conceptions of the mind, the *ego*, the soul, the universe, of karma and of reincarnation are formed, and thus an endless chain of conceptions is created, which not a single ancient philosophy or religion, or modern psychology for that matter, is devoid of. True, at first these conceptions do come in handy to guide the seeker towards the Path, to give him direction and to set a tentative target.

However, if the searcher is only engaged in theories that are not supported by systematic practical discipline, they function counterproductively, creating tremendous conflict, frustration and confusion in the seeker's mind, enslaving him with even more force than this rough instinctive-sensorial world that is filled with unawakened wishes and affects.

However, if we search for the one who is experiencing the experience of all these conceptions through the simple practice of questioning the true nature of our being, we will not find him. If we look for *the mind's and the ego's* sources, we will see that it does not exist. If we honestly delve ourselves into our inner selves and ask: "*Who is the person that is searching?*" we will see that our seeker disappears, that he is just a figment of our imagination.

In reality all that exists are the functions of universal Consciousness, such as: *memory, will, feeling, thinking* and *perception*, that appear as being seemingly separated from their substance due to the universal will's movement through the individual being. And the dynamics of the will's continuous changes is a *process*, not a *substance*.

Neither the body, nor mind, nor *His Majesty* the self-appointed *ego* exists as a distinct and separate substance or an individual being. The only and absolute substance that exists is the universal *Being-Consciousness-Bliss* (Sat-Chit-Ananda). All of creation is nothing more than Universal consciousness's and will's game, the static and dynamic aspect of the one and the same Reality, while the mind, the world and the *ego* are a mere delusion, just a mirage with which the *cosmic game (maya)* seduces the slumbering and the dreaming, the drowsy and the unawoken. If only we were to give up on all these overrated conceptions, our will would naturally return to its source, free of all the obstacles that constantly create the ego's insatiable ambition.

The tragicomedy of the *walking paradox* called man is that there is no obstacle that he cannot overcome, under the condition that he gives up the ambition that welcomes every new running start of his by raising the bar. If this paradox were completely seen through, is there anyone who would continue to languish like the prisoner of an invisible prison?

V.7 Awoken Reality or *the blink of actualization*

Every morning when we wake up, we do not wake up in instalments. We do not try to wake up, we simply wake up when we're done dreaming our dreams. The same applies to the Path. We come into being, or more precisely, we are made present in our reality the moment that we lose all reasons to continue to feed illusions.

All the methods to the Path of Self-Knowledge serve no purpose other than to create for the seeker the opportunity for the freeing leap into the moment, into his *here and now*. This is the moment in which the wall between *the I and the other*, between the inner and the outer world falls, and the differences between consciousness and its conditions disappear.

Actualization is the moment: man liberates himself when he realizes that time is an illusion, because eternity and temporality, wakefulness and sleep, consciousness and illusion cannot exist in parallel. Every morning when we wake up, we do not wake up in instalments. We do not try to wake up, we simply wake up when we're done dreaming our dreams. The same applies to the Path. We come into being, or more precisely, we *are made present in our reality* the moment that we lose all reasons to continue to feed illusions.

When we understand this, we realize that that time and space are nothing but an illusion of the mind, and that *Awakening* is a quantum leap from the artificially regulated, routinely predictable regime of life to a completely different, unpredictable, spontaneous, flowing *conscious life.*

In this context, the "eternity" we can personally experience is just a moment. And that is the whole reality. The past exists only in our memory, the future only in our imagination. Both past and future are only the categories of the mind. And the only reality we can empirically experience is this moment, *here and now.* We cannot even say that this moment is eternal. It is timeless.

Our True Being is an authentic expression of this timeless reality. It is a pure, undivided, *self-enlightening consciousness* in which there is no ignorance and delusion, disease and suffering. All doubts and confusion come only from two things: from memories of and attachment to the past and a projected future based on those memories. Given that both are baseless and unreal, memory and projection can exist only in the mind.

The mind that is stimulated to action through these mechanical and unconscious impulses of the memory divides the moment into before and after, it divides space into here and elsewhere, it divides the world into mine and yours, and finally, it divides itself into *being and being described.* And so ultimately the mind also divides our True Being into the Self *that it is* and the ego it *wants to be*, into a clean the mirror and the fake reflection in it, which in its delusion it identifies with, into the Self that it has forgotten and the *image of itself* that it builds and supports with its every activity... and defends to the last moment.

Consequently, all true paths to self-knowledge aspire to tear down further withdrawal for the mind (or ego, as you like) and shorten the retreat before the confrontation with oneself. All true paths actually lead the ego to the abyss. And that is why man frees himself of the mind's delusions and the ego's tyranny only when he has no other way out, when the only remaining option is to jump into the Emptiness of undivided being in which there no longer is any support for its dreams and illusions.

Actualization is but a moment of realization, of making present that opportunity and this immense potential that sleeps in the deep sleep of every unawoken being. And reality is that very moment of takeoff, that very jump that bridges the chasm between potency and act, between the "primate" and the man that has roused all his dormant potential.

This moment is just a reflection of the timeless, the jump is a reflection of the absolute, and the awakening just the blink of the forever Awoken. Before and after that blink, there is but dreaming that is not worth mentioning, let alone be written about...

VI. HOW TO LOOSEN THE JAWS OF THE DOG THAT HAS FIRMLY BITTEN INTO THE FOG

The "ego" subdues and kills: it operates like an organic cell: it is a robber and it is violent. It wants to regenerate itself – pregnancy. It wants to give birth to its god and see all mankind at his feet.

Friedrich Nietzsche: The Will to Power

Since in truth, bondage and freedom are relative, these words are only for those terrified of the universe. This universe is a reflection of minds. As you see many suns in water from one sun, so see bondage and liberation.

Vijnana Bhairava Tantra: one of the

main texts of Kashmir Shaivism

VI.1 The struggle for power: the dominant and the submissive patterns of *energy economy*

This I, which is founded on conditioned relationships fulfilled by comparison, competition and the struggle for dominance, is not the true Self. This is the false I or ego. And since the ego has no foundation in itself, all that it has, the ego has in relation to others. The ego simply, metaphorically speaking, hits or provo-

kes hits in order to draw attention to itself: "Look at me, here I am, accept me no matter what I do!"

There is nothing more difficult than to become and be *I*, especially since every effort of development and maturation in that direction faces opposition from *others* who, protecting their own position in relation to *you*, always *know what's best* for you and how you should really be.

Until man has realized and founded himself in that *true I*, he does not yet *have a Self*, he does not know who he belongs to, but he wants to belong to someone because it is difficult to live without belonging; that is, until you are able to really to *be I!* And this is how in man's initial effort to mature, to *be I*, is countered by the resistance of the *other ego*, which establishes, protects and confirms itself on account of every *rival I*, regardless of whether it has a relationship based on kinship, partnership, business or friendship with it.

This *I*, which is founded on conditioned relationships fulfilled by comparison, competition and the struggle for dominance, is not the *true self*. This is the false I or ego. And since the ego has no foundation in itself, all that it has, the ego has in relation to *others*. The ego simply, metaphorically speaking, hits or provokes hits in order to draw attention to itself: *"Look at me, here I am, accept me no matter what I do!"*

If we sift through all the strategies that the ego uses in his fight for power and status, for possession and domination, we will notice two key patterns which come up: *the dominant and the submissive*. The first is based on the possession of the other person through physical, emotional or intellectual submission and economic, political or ideological repression, and in each of these forms of domination there lies a moral and spiritual subjugation because the ego, as it confirms itself, denies the moral autonomy and spiritual identity of the other person.

In principle, any relationship between two *ego* is unconsciously dictated by the *principle of energy economy*, which most people are not even aware of. But what does that actually mean? Since the ego has no direct contact with its own sources of vital energy which is repressed by and tied to the defensive structures in the psyche's unconscious (or better said, unawakened) fields, it needs the energy of other beings much like we need the bread that feeds us, and it gets it using the tried and true tactics that have been employed throughout centuries. And as was said, all these strategies can be reduced to the two sides of a tested pattern, *by hook or by crook.*

The other, submissive type of the *ego's* scramble for energy uses the inverted, twisted side of the battle for power and dominance. Faced with a physically, emotionally or intellectually superior opponent, the submissive personality type realizes that it cannot get energy and the satisfaction that it seeks in a dominant fashion. It therefore only seemingly accepts the superior partner's dominance of the game in order draw him in, make him dependent on its *support* and finally blackmail him with its own *availability.*

Of course, such a relationship creates a morbidly complex addictive relationship between two immature and dependent personalities, because the supposed *superiority* feeds on the other's submissiveness, and personal *submissiveness* compensates with the partner's superiority.

However, in the long-run both strategies prevent the individual from developing into a psychologically independent, morally autonomous and spiritually self-confident person who finds life energy and spiritual inspiration on the path of self--development within itself.

VI.2 No one can own the one who appropriates nothing

We can only reach our authentic I am through the rejection of all forms of (social and psychological) relations: to possess or to be possessed! That is why a true man of the Path cannot be owned by anyone, because he himself does not claim anything for himself.

The man who was not able to fight his rivals *for himself*, who took the path of least resistance, who repressed himself or who modelled himself according to the criteria of others in order to be accepted by this environment, has lost himself on the path of development towards *becoming I* and must once again start from where he left off, from where he got lost, to once again find himself.

In the two previously described models of the *ego's* scramble for energy, the dominant and the submissive, *having* is a replacement for *being*. The dominant type has to assume power through the economic, emotional, etc. possession of others for it to know it exists. The submissive type must attract the attention of others (for the place where we focus our attention is also where our energy is concentrated), even at the cost of losing its independence, in order for it to exist.

But all these strategies that *manipulate through energy*, (our own as well as our environment's), lead us astray from our real goal, *to be the I which I am*! All these sidetracks lead only to the slavery known as *having an ego*. This, in short, boils down to the game of *possessing or being possessed*. And the ego is the most callous slaveholder seen since Caligula.

The ego is an infinitely cruel master because it feeds on the boundless indifference of the unawakened pole of our being, our mental *Shadow*. Where there is no consciousness there is no conscience, and where there is no conscience, life is just a mechanical chew, a bestial struggle for energy resources, a perfidious "grub" to the shortest and most efficient way to transform others' protein into one's own.

We can only reach our authentic *I am* through the rejection of all forms of (social and psychological) relations: *to possess or to be possessed*! That is why a *true man of the Path* cannot be owned by anyone, because he himself does not claim anything for himself. As long as he dwells on the egocentric horizontal of *having*, any individual is dependent on *the other*. But when he straightens up into the vertical of *being*, he becomes self-sufficient because he realizes that nothing really exists except for the *Self* or the true Self.

The intersection of the horizontal and vertical represents the cross of our existence on which the *illusory ego* was crucified, or where the *Son of Man* was crucified between *having and being*. However, the biggest and most difficult transparent paradox of this mental crucifixion is that the cross is also a catapult for the spiritual liberation of our True Being or for the *Son of God*.

Why then was this messenger who was sent to this world to communicate this deep secret (in the most direct way as his path is direct and precipitous) so cruelly punished? Because *others* do not need us when we are in possession of our *authentic Self*. Others only need us as an embodiment of the projection of their desires, only as a shadow of their visions, only as an object of their needs. The other's ego rejects you when it is approached with *your I*, because in its selfishness, there is no room for two subjects.

If you fall into the trap of your *having* or of your need to be accepted, you will never find your I. You will become modeling clay in the hands of the other. When the other is tired of playing, it will discard you in the same way worn-out toys are discarded.

Only the liberated, developed I can choose between *self--sufficient solitude* and *harmonious community* without a dependency on others. And only a union between two mature person has the strength to survive, because deep within their hearts they know they are not *two* but One.

VI.3 Existence is simply a struggle for energy

Viewed from the prevailing perspective of the average unawakened specimen of the human species, most relationships between human beings are an unconscious, instinctive struggle for ener-

gy resources, a true energy trade which in extreme cases ends in fraud, extortion and robbery.

Existence is a struggle for power. All living species try to turn the proteins of other species into their own in order to survive. And that is the Earth's law of survival.

If we understand "proteins" as being the unit representing the necessary *energy sources* at all levels of human existence (physical, emotional, mental and spiritual), it will be clear that any being that is not able to secure its own supplies of energy must seek energy in another being. That is why all of evolution moves towards all the more developed forms of life as *flowing energy sources.*

At the rough, material level of existence, various life forms (herbivores, carnivores and omnivores) assimilate others' energy through food. At more subtle levels of existence, the emotions of others represent very delicate energy sources. At the mental level of existence, someone's thoughts, ideas, visions become a sort of (better or worse quality) food.

Finally, we come to the purest energy sources at the most refined level of existence, and that is pure awareness of our spiritual being. But these extremely subtle energy vibrations, which are emitted by spiritually enlightened persons such as saints, sages and spiritual teachers, can only be perceived and assimilated by a very small number of people who have purified their consciousness to those depths.

Unfortunately, in Western civilization there is no collective cultural consciousness that would point to the extreme importance of the careful selection of the emotional, mental and spiritual food that people unconsciously ingest. The amount of attention that is exclusively paid to physical nutrition demonstrates how materialistic Western civilization is in its narcissistic cult of the body; nutrition and similar costly disciplines that deal with food for the body are booming.

But how much systematic research in Western societies has been conducted in order to prove that the food with which we feed our mind and our soul, i. e. the kind of music we listen to, the books we read, the movies we watch; that the content we consume through mentally aggressive and morally prostituted mass media, is equally, if not even more important?

For the creators of all that cultural, subcultural and quasi-cultural content slip us their own good visions, inspiration and positive incentives as well as their traumas, neuroses and perversions. Food manufacturers (material, emotional or mental) and their mostly unconscious consumers are but the two ends of the energy chain.

There are many more links in this chain (distributors, managers and marketers, the media and advertising industry) that live off this travesty of a symbiotic system like leeches. This is a system that survives only because nine-tenths of humanity does not know that it has its own inexhaustible supply of energy and doesn't know how to establish an open channel with its own power source.

Viewed from the prevailing perspective of the average unawakened specimen of the human species, most relationships between human beings are an unconscious and instinctive struggle for energy resources, a true energy trade which in extreme cases ends in fraud, extortion and robbery.

The person that you have "hooked" yourself to in the inert search for energy actually imperceptibly draws and steals your own energy, and vice versa. "Love", which is of sentimental or erotic character as it is mostly superficially promoted in western civilization's pop culture, is mainly a mimicry in these relationships that serves to more easily open the "victim's" psychic defensive structure. And in the rare situations and relationships where true, unselfish, uncalculating love (or better said, *empathy*) is at work, these are actually spiritual vibrations that the vast majority of *mortals* on this planet simply cannot sense.

As we said, such vibrations are emitted by spiritually purified or even enlightened people. There have never been many such people, and the question is how many diligent followers they can permanently attract. And of these *diligent* followers, how many loyal students can they keep around themselves? Of these *loyal* followers, how many true devotees can they rise to their own level or lead to the end point of human evolution, to enlightenment?

In comparison to the tremendous demographic expansion of the human species today, these numbers are negligible. That is why each individual is called to direct himself to search for his own source of consciousness/energy through contemplation and self-knowledge.

Because ultimately, though most people in their ignorance crave *meat*, emotions and ideas, every one slowly but surely, more or less consciously, turns towards the Source of all *resources* in the end, to their own Being.

VI.4 The will for power over the object of desire

In this contest against its objects, the personal, individual will exhausts itself little by little because the world of objects, like the world desire, is inexhaustible until the will realizes that in truth it cannot permanently possess anyone or anything, not even Itself, until it gives up its desire to possess.

Unconscious ego is a raw will for power. This will is expressed in different ways at various degrees of awareness: as the child's will to master its motor skills, as the adolescent's will to impose himself to his environment, as the young man's will to master the object of his erotic desires while avoiding the situation in which his *ego* will be overwhelmed by the object's will or by the power of its own desires.

Finally, it is expressed as the mature man's will to rule "his world" exactly as he experiences it, whether it be a question of family, business or any kind of engagement that his unconscious *ego* fulfills, identifies or confirms itself with. However, such a will is necessarily contradicted by its environment's will, that experiences this intrusive, unconscious *ego* as being aggressively competitive insofar as it refuses to adapt to the demands of its milieu.

In this early conflict between the unconscious will for power and the social environment's demands as a type of *superego*, the young being will necessarily begin to form a so-called *conscious ego* (as the organization center of its own personality) which primarily and precisely serves to satisfy its unconscious will (which Freud called the *libido*), but in such a way as to avoid a conflict with the superior social and familial superego.

This kind of *double-satisfaction* strategy, of one's own and of social authority's will, necessarily develops a center of the conscious part of the psyche which is already formed as a split, *ambivalent I* in the process where it becomes autonomous. Namely, such an I imposes itself as both the controller of and opponent to the psyche's unconscious pole (in Jungian terms the *Shadow*), experiencing it as its dark and inert, often wild and uncultivated, and in every way non-integrated side and consequently as a kind of rival *non-ego*.

Their conflict will last until the Shadow "gives up" its will to power, and the ego its obsessive control. However, the psyche's two split poles cannot resign themselves from their unconscious impulses until leadership in the psychological integration process (or in the re-establishment of a unified functional psychological whole) is taken over by the center of a whole, undivided Consciousness or Self (German: *Selbst* is the term used by C. G. Jung which in analytical psychology refers to the real center of psychic organization, but also to the psyche as a whole).

Only the unique, undivided I is able to see that the repressive *superego*, disguised as social, cultural and spiritual authorities and assimilated dogmas and prohibitions, is but the reverse side of the deeply repressed and rigidly controlled drives of the unconscious will to be, to possess, to sustain and feed oneself with the energy of the self-subjected will of its environment.

Each will strives for the object of its desire until it overpowers it. And when it overpowers it, it rejects it like a cat rejects a dead mouse because the game is no longer interesting. This predatory *game of will and object* is most graphically manifested in the battle of the sexes, whether in mere flirtation, seduction or partner relationship. That is why this battle is, while it is un-awakened, instinctively ruthless; because the first to bow down before the will of the stronger partner often becomes the help-less prey, victim or toy of its archaic predatory instincts.

But on the other hand, there are also different, more subtle strategies available to the ego that has established that it can-not control the chosen object *with its will*. In this case, the seemingly *defeated ego* can only ostensibly subdue itself to its partner to perfidiously control it with its susceptibility and make the partner's self-love dependent on its support. The insightful observer is not blind to the fact that in such partner-ships, an unusual but effective psychological symbiosis reigns, in which *the leader from the outside follows on the inside, the follower from the outside leads on the inside.*

That is why the will of every unconscious person naturally strives to either impose itself on or to submit itself to the stronger will. If its aspiration is satisfied in no way, the uncon-scious will goes in search of a new object of desire. This quest can lead all the way to *God Himself* as a supernatural, trans-cendent object of the unconscious will's. This is confirmed by the observation that this will, in its relationship to God, acts in one of the two, tried and true ways.

At first it tries to master using God's (or transcendent) power, through a variety of *magical* rites and practices. When such an approach proves itself to be counterproductive, and sooner or later it always does because you cannot "do trade" with *transcendence* as the totality of existence (Jung would say, as a *psychic totality*) like a petty trader working from a cheap stand; personal will then takes a condescending attitude towards the more superior, *transpersonal Will*. This represents a key crossover from a magical to a *mystical* relationship with God, embodied by the evangelical saying "Father, thy will be done!"

In this contest against its objects, the personal, individual will exhausts itself little by little because the world of objects, like the world of desire, is inexhaustible until will realizes that in truth it cannot permanently possess anyone or anything, not even Itself, until it gives up its desire to possess. Said in mystical language: only when the personal will renounces *its ego*, when it *immerses itself in its non-ego* can it merge with its own, transcendent Source (or Absolute Subject) and experience the state of transpersonal unity, the state of ultimate fulfillment in the *fullness of existence* (Greek: pleroma) which all beings unconsciously yearn for.

This whole evolutionary movement of the unawakened, unintegrated will, from the simplest to the most advanced forms of life or objects of its desire, is but the individual's unconscious expression of desire for union with the Absolute. But that's an area that goes far beyond the area of psychology, which enters the field of *meta-psychology*, or to be precise, falls into the language of the undefined area of *mysticism* which we can experience only when we abandon the framework of language and the limits of intellect.

VI.5 How to loosen the jaws of the dog that has firmly bitten into the fog?

Over time, we see that desire grows and flourishes in proportion to the power of control and repression, in such a way that this neurotic circuit unconsciously and automatically locks into an almost unbreakable chain of adhesion, control and linkage. Desire, fear and anger support each other, and like the three legs of a tripod, they meet at one point, control, which the ego identifies with, both as the jailor and the prisoner.

Meditation allows us to gradually awaken our earliest childhood experiences. It helps us to understand how the *inner conflicts* in which we are entangled were woven. If we are patient and awake enough, we will come to the realization that craving, or the mind's adherence to the phenomena that it *unconsciously* manifests, is the main source of the neurotic pitfalls in which the ego is involved, both as its engineer and as its victim.

Namely, the stronger the craving is, the greater fear and anxiety it causes: whether it be from the loss of the object of desire, or because of social prohibitions in terms of reaching for the object of desire, or because of *separation from the Self* (or splitting the Being's authentic unity), that winning over the object of desire requires. The fear that appears as an obstacle to desire causes frustration and gives birth to the anger that seeks the demolition of obstacles and prohibitions that come from both external authorities and internal, assimilated taboos.

But since from the youngest age we see that all authoritarian community, from family to school to broader social institutions and ultimately to the State, do not support but rather severely punish the spontaneous expression of anger, we learn various strategies of anger control on our own, and thus learn to control our desires and fears as well.

Over time, we see that desire grows and flourishes in proportion to the power of control and repression, in such a way that this neurotic circuit unconsciously and automatically locks into an almost unbreakable *chain of adhesion, control and linkage.* Desire, fear and anger support each other and, like the three legs of a tripod, they meet at one point, *control*, which the ego identifies with, both as the jailor and the prisoner.

"Control" has become a mass model and a life burden instead of the spontaneity, authenticity and natural simplicity which we carry in ourselves as the True Being; this is why sex has become so overrated. This is because sex is one of the few areas in which people can express their repressed anger which is mixed with desire and fears without being punished for it by social authorities. But by engaging in this kind of sex, people do not realize that instead of solving the problem they simply *transfer it from the social to the intimate dimension.*

Unconsciously assimilating forms of social repression, although they seem to resist society's demand, unawakened people do not see that they continue to *punish* themselves and their partners in neurotic relationships. Thus sex turns into a perverse game of mutual punishment and self-punishment.

All the repressed pain, fear and aggression that people cannot manifest to social authorities is projected onto their loved ones, onto their partners and children. And so instead of giving those people the best of themselves, they end up giving them the worst. This is a victory for ancient social repression over the individual which is re-confirmed and a further guaranteed until the individual decides to wake up and take the chains of centuries of deception off himself.

Often this "nagging" our loved ones is accompanied by feelings of guilt that further stimulate the neurotic game of the exchange of punishment and self-punishment. Through rather *pathetic family relationships*, the game turns into a pathological sadomasochism that is camouflaged by deceptive farces, in which the lack of true love masks itself through the duty and the possessiveness through a great love, and the sick *transfer* is masked with special attachment.

This is most often the unawakened *chain of adhesion, control and linkage* which arises out of the sheer unconsciousness and spiritual ignorance in which people blunder like a dog *that has firmly bitten into the fog* and who is growling, writhing around, thrashing, not knowing how to open his jaws and *simply let go...*

Therefore, the only safe and responsible way people can *let go of obsessive control* and loosen the jaws that bite others and themselves is not sex, but meditation. When they practically come to realize this and integrate it into their daily lives, sex then loses its overrated importance and meditation becomes *love instead of sex.*

However, as it is easy to misunderstand things and to confuse concepts when people accept certain assumptions without a practical test, it should be noted that meditation is not merely a substitute for sex. It is not a surrogate; it is the natural, original state of our Being, and is in itself sufficient.

But on the other hand, it does not exclude sex from the individual's life; rather, it helps him develop good relationships filled with consciousness and love and not compulsive, neurotic and pathological relationships that are filled with bitterness, guilt and (self)punishment.

VI.6. While looking out – one can see only their own reflection

If we convince ourselves that ego is an illusion, and fight with it at the same time as if it were real, then we have a disastrous paradox, a condition we have already described as a mad dog that has firmly bitten a fog... It is a condition in which a rigid and unflexible traveller easily goes astray, it can lead him to neurosis, often even to a deep psychological regression.

By looking at himself in the mirror, a person thinks he sees himself whereas in reality he sees only his own reflection. Since his mind has been long conditioned to observe the external and does not see the internal – the space he observes from, he easily confuses illusion and reality. In a nutshell, a person forgets that he is – *The one who sees*, and everything he sees – is merely His reflection.

All impressions and reflections he has stored in his memory are threads used for weaving the shroud of his *false-I*. Even when he manages to comprehend it, he cannot easily untie their *knot* which lies deeply in the collective unconscious. However, he can cease to identify with them. Then, the veil of illusions will drop by itself, and what is left is the face of the Unborn who has been watching the drama of the world since time immemorial...

The main misapprehension a traveller gives up the hardest is a naive but strong conviction that there is such a thing as *ego*... and that casting away ego leads to freedom. Such a conviction can have several objections. Firstly, if we accept the idea that ego exists, there is a question of who is aware of its existence. If a seeker replies that he is the one who is aware – that leads us to another question: How can he simultaneously be – The one who is aware and the ego he is aware of?

If we muse upon this question in contemplation, with time we will see that the relationship between *the observer* and *the seen* – is as bogus as a dream. We will understand that the observer who identified himself with the seen is merely a dreamer, and ego is just a role in his dream. In other words, while dreaming, we are only aware of the dream, but not of ourselves. Once we wake up, we become aware of ourselves, and the dream is looked through the fog of memories which is slowly disappearing. Do we ask ourselves when we wake up: *Is the dream an illusion we need to cast away?* No!

We simply wake up and forget the dream as something unreal. The same principle goes for a psychological phenomenon – ego. It is simply *the dream of myself.* Once we become aware of Ourselves – do we know then who we are and we do not need surrogates of dreams anymore.

Since there are two sides to every phenomenon, and so is with this one. If we convince ourselves that ego is an illusion, and fight with it at the same time as if it were real, then we have a disastrous paradox, a condition we have already described as *a mad dog that has firmly bitten a fog...* It is a condition in which a rigid and unflexible traveller easily goes astray, it can lead him to neurosis, often even to a deep psychological regression.

What can the traveller do when on his Path encountered by such an impenetrable psychological nimbus? The only thing he can do in such a situation is – remember Himself, come back to the observer's state and cease to identify with projections of the mind which are nothing but shadows of memories. Maybe in that impartial observation he can take advantage of the given opportunity to discover what the real basis in the core of all those nonexistent and tricky mental conditions is. But that is, of course, possible only if the traveller used a disciplined practice of contemplation and developed a habit in which in stressful situations he does not react with *inertia* but *with presence*. Only then can he timely *remember Himself*, at the right moment become aware of *here and now*. Then, he can possibly understand that efforts to cast away ego are illusionary and counterproductive because they come from the state of non-understanding, from the essence of ego, and they make ego even stronger instead of making it weaker.

Therefore, ego does not need repressive reins but understanding and awareness. When we become aware of what ego is and understand the way it works, ego is not a problem anymore but a solution. It is not a trap but the tools for setting oneself free. As we have already mentioned before, ego is just a transit phase in the development of consciousness, from the unconscious to the pure, unconditioned consciousness. It is a temporary centre which will, once it fulfills its role, give way on this Path to our deeper centre. So the key problem is not ego itself but its position in our psychic scheme. As the Moon does not have its own shining but it reflects the light of the sun, so ego only reflects the light of Self – so that the mind illusioned by the world can once search for the source of that evershining light.

Once we realize ego is nothing stable, something we need to get rid of, we will understand that *the magic of liberation lies in the fact we need to stop supporting it.* Then it will fall off by itself.

VI.7 The four types of transformation of the mind: Four paths to True Power

These four qualities of the purified mind: service, dedication, wisdom and presence, turn the mind from the selfish ego to the Being's center and the real Source of power, from which springs our creative potential, our capacity for cognition and self-reflection, as well as the trail that takes us back to our original identity.

All beings crave power because it is a prerequisite for their survival. It means even more to the ego as power is a means of self-affirmation. Or simply put, without power *there is no* ego. Even very young children, in the early stage of development, instinctively try to impose their will on their environment; their unconscious desire for power.

Mastering its environment, circumstances, people around it, in the end mastering itself and its resources is every "ego's" primary drive. However, each *ego* does not reach its goal the same way. If, through the basic functions of the mind, we can divide people into willful, emotional and intellectual types, we can also discern at least as many paths to power.

Willful types try to win and impose their power through the potency of their will. Emotional types achieve this in a more subtle and indirect fashion; they use a whole network of emotional manipulation, attempting to make others dependent on them and thus gain power over them. For intellectual types, the path to power is knowledge. For thinkers, gaining power over others means knowing more than them or having, at any cost, an exclusive opinion on everything.

Each of these types instinctively tries to draw power from others in its own way, drawing their attention at the same time because attention is energy and energy is power. Even the baby in a cradle, still deeply unconscious, tries by all available means to draw the attention of its surroundings because attention is just as necessary to its survival as are air and food.

There is a fourth type of person, observers. They refuse to get involved in the world of human relationships; whether through an imposition of their will, through the exchange of feelings, through taking open positions on anything or through a clear court decision. They naturally try to accumulate and absorb power "from themselves" through careful, watchful observation. Therefore, in principle, they are not tied to other people, but primarily to themselves. This is how they develop a very sophisticated form of selfishness. In order to accumulate and preserve their own sources of power they are constantly cautious, keeping an invisible but high wall between themselves and other people.

However, regardless of the technique, every ego is actually a selfish *self-feeding through the energy of power* mechanism. Given that the mechanisms for controlling its own resources are insufficient due to its defensive structures, the ego automatically searches for *victims* from which it can deplete more energy. Since every potential victim has its own conscious or unconscious energy absorption mechanism, people mutually feed on and exhaust one another. Their mutual relations, no matter how much they *vibrate* under the hypocritical guise of idealism at first, eventually become a *naked battle for power* when they are bare of all deceit.

In their quest for power, unconscious people emotionally seduce each other, create a family, have children, so that their partners and descendant can stimulate and revitalize their personal power. In their selfish dream they do not see that they actually deplete each other and that more or less all interpersonal relationships are unconsciously based on the predatory *struggle for power*. Sex is just one of the most explicit forms of that primordial struggle. That's the fundamental reason why sex will never give people the permanent fulfillment of any desire; because sexual instinct rises from the predatory desire to subjugate the other to one's own power and to seize his power, not give him power.

Everyone is involved in this struggle for power: lovers, spouses, parents and children, brothers and sisters, friends and partners of all kinds. Energy is exchanged at all mental levels: willful, emotional, intellectual and observational. Most often partners are chosen according to those criteria.

As it is more difficult for the willful type to impose his power on other willful types, he will target the emotional, intellectual or observational type. Since similar types deal with similar mechanisms for the struggle for power, competition between them can become too exhausting. Therefore, they search for partners that complement them, looking for the quality which they personally lack most in the other.

For example, the willful type who is constantly ready for action, which can be a constant source of stress, will readily seek the relaxing company of the emotional type. The emotional type is prone to inertia and often seeks the willful type's driving force or the intellectual type's lucid inspiration. The indecisive intellectual type, who is often prone to divergent internal conflicts, may seek the emotional support of the emotional type or the decisiveness and agency of the willful type.

All the types will instinctively seek the presence of the observer because, seemingly passive, he seems to be the ideal victim for the *imposition of power*. However, what the other types do not understand, and what the careful observer will never tell them, is the simple fact that the observer is the one who choses and takes or rejects since he is the least dependent on others. Since he best knows how to economize his own energy resources, he is the most self-sufficient, and in a certain way, the most selfish.

Just like the ego draws its power from the environment through the four functions of the mind, the True Being can open the door to direct access to power through the four types of *transformation of the mind*, but only to that one power that transcends individual resources. This is the creative power of the Source which is the root of all beings, but it cannot be given to the ego's selfish interests. Moreover, the ego cannot receive, because its controls and defenses close the path to the

Source. These doors that give direct access to power open at the moment when man gives up the *desire for power* and when he allows himself to be filled and taken by the *power of love*. But renunciation and consent are not possible until the ego is cleansed to the point of selflessness, and that is when True Nature takes up the Path.

Each personality type has to be purified through the positive *complement* of the function of the mind that he used as a manipulation medium on his loved ones. Thus the uncleansed willful type, who is usually a selfish bully, must purify himself through selfless work; the emotional manipulator through unconditional and uncalculated love; the speculator through the acquisition and sharing of knowledge for the common good; the ignorant observer, who through reservation distances himself from others, must purify himself through openness for compassion. He must learn *to be there for others*, without the expectation of getting anything in return, besides opening his own *preserved* heart.

Then, selfish wills transforms into service, selfish feelings to devotion, selfish reasoning to practical wisdom, and selfish aloofness to compassionate presence. These four qualities of the purified mind, *service, dedication, wisdom and presence*, turn the mind from the selfish ego, who under all circumstances sought the power to determine and protect itself, to the Being's center and the real Source of power, from which springs our creative potential, our capacity for cognition and self-reflection, as well as the trail that takes us back to our original identity.

True power or the *Spirit's power* descends on man only when there is no more "selfish ego" to appropriate and *capi-*

talize on it. Only when the Spirit can hand power over to the purified Being in order to give to all those in need through it because spiritual power is never given to selfish interests. While the ego leads the game of life, man is "appropriated" by that inner *demon* who exhausts it until the drives him mad or kills him in the end.

When the True Being takes the lead, when man is released from his monstrous and unnatural, frantic obsession with the ego, he becomes a *liberated man*, not only for himself but first and foremost to serve his spiritual mission; in fact, the only one that he really came to this world for, the reason why he treads the world from which he will not depart until his mission is fulfilled, no matter how many times he must go back to it.

VII. THE PASSAGE THROUGH THE DECEPTIVE VEIL OF ILLUSION

The object is an object for the subject,
The subject is a subject for the object:
Know that the relativity of the two
Rests ultimately on one Emptiness.

Seng Ts'an: Hsin Hsin Ming (Faith in Mind)

Third patriarch of Zen Buddhism

This world with all its living beings and inanimate objects is nothing more than a creation of the mind. When the mind's activities cease there is no world or duality.

Gaudapada: Gaudapada Karika,

central text in the teachings of Advaita Vedanta

VII.1 The passage through the deceptive veil of illusion

If in deep contemplation we look at that which we call the mind, we will see that it is a myriad of waves which follow one another in rapid stream of consciousness; that it is millions of infinitely fast vibrations which through mutual play build up a virtual reality which, by means of upbringing, education and the habit of insight-deprived criticism, have been accepted as something real and based on steady legalities.

The ego is viewed as an entity that is separate and opposed to the world only when we nourish and support it through the investment of the mental energy that we project in it in the form of thoughts, feelings, desires, drive, ambition... Through such an unconscious, conditioned and learned support we allow these clusters of accumulated impressions to thicken, condense into a separate, seemingly autonomous entity and to take control of our life.

However, through disciplined contemplation, we can destroy that phantom, destroy the mental cocoon that captures us and alienates us from a free life, destroys the cloud of ignorance that muddies a potentially clear vision of reality as well as our True Nature.

For contemplation restores the energy that is necessary for the ego's self-preservation from a state of bondage to accumulated sensory, emotional or mental impressions to a state of pure uninterrupted consciousness/energy flow which in fact is just like the state of our True Nature.

Figuratively speaking, contemplation directly allows us to see that an enchanting natural phenomenon such as a waterfall is actually an illusion; that the waterfall does not actually exist, that it is in fact millions of drops consecutively and separately falling, however, the mind, which connects the ultra-short sequences of perception in a continuum, recognizes it as a separate and distinct phenomenon.

The deluded mind treats external phenomena the same way it treats its so-called mindset. If in deep contemplation we look at that which we call the mind, we will see that it is a myriad of waves which follow one another in rapid stream of consciousness; that it is millions of infinitely fast vibrations which through mutual play build up a virtual reality which, by means of upbringing, education and the habit of insight-deprived criticism, have been accepted as something real and based on steady legalities.

In reality, it couldn't be anything further from that, because our mindset (as our scientific and technocratic civilization understands and defines it) is no more than a figment of our imagination whose source, to make the matters worse, is yet to be found. The same goes for the ego: it is an imaginary entity's millions of attributes that our mind alternatively stores and retrieves from its memory archives in order to have some sort of personal identity in its faceless and transpersonal existence.

Therefore, despite all scientific theorems and experimentally validated models, only contemplation allows pure unconditioned consciousness (chit) to see a passage through the mind's misleading network of thoughts, impressions and concepts which form the thick veil of illusion, and in one lightning-fast flash of awakening pierce through into freedom from all self-delusions.

> *How is the veil to stand*
> *without you holding it up?*
> *Do not demand, do not expect and that*
> *primordial reality will suddenly appear.*

VII.2 Cultivating consciousness is beyond reason and intellect's strategies

Even though it hides all our spiritual and enlightening potential in its embryo, the Path cannot blossom until we abandon the double-layered cocoon of illusion, woven from commonsensical faith in the sensory world and intellectual confidence in the world of abstract concepts.

The difference between reason and intellect is akin to the difference between tacticians and strategists. Reason is practical, it does not bother with definitive answers; it searches for a solution to a concrete problem and it develops with experience. But its boundaries are determined by the givens of sensory experience because it is entirely dependent on them.

Intellect is conceptual, it seeks final and universal answers; it is not satisfied with concrete and sporadic solutions; it searches for general principles. It does not rely on sensory experience and it develops through learning and reflection.

While the tactical reason rules in the limited field of small conflicts and battles, the strategic intellect envisages winning wars. However, both functions of our relative and conditioned mind are limited and mutually dependent. To overcome their limitations, it is necessary to activate the function that simultaneously balances and transcends them: consciousness.

Consciousness understands concrete problems without depending on the senses and sees the basic principles without depending on acquired theoretical concepts. At the same time, transcending any division of consciousness into aspects and functions that were detected, defined and catalogued by our discriminative mind, consciousness works instantly and without advance planning, and spontaneously responds to life's challenges, adapting to the requirements of the given circumstances.

It is not acquired through life experience or academic education because it is innate, but in order for it to be activated out of its sleepy inertia, for it to be awoken and be involved in daily life, what is necessary is discipline. This discipline is the cultivation of attention or consciousness that evolves in three stages:

I. Concentration (gathering scattered and wandering attention);

II. Meditation (reflection on the nature of the mind and of the ego through self-analysis that is performed through concentrated attention);

III. Contemplation (pure unmotivated observation of all outward appearances and inner states, towards which consciousness acts as a mirror that reflects their interdependence, but does not adopt or reject them).

The third and highest level of cultivation of attention actualizes that state of consciousness which in Buddhism is called adarshana-jnana. This term could be translated as self-reflecting consciousness or unlearned mirrored knowledge. Therefore, it is the original, undifferentiated consciousness that grasps and understands phenomena, not through sensory-intellectual analysis but through purely intuitive (self)reflection.

This means that consciousness gains knowledge on phenomena directly in pure contemplation, rather than through experimentation, studying and reasoning. Therefore, such knowledge is called unlearned knowledge or direct insight into the essence of things. This is possible because the consciousness and phenomena are based on the same quality and thus interdependent. It is only intellect, through conceptual definitions, that divides them, characterizes them as isolated, mutually independent phenomena and archives them as such into purely abstract categories.

Once we experience this in practice, we will understand that the Path's philosophy, or the philosophy of self-knowledge, is neither empirical nor speculative, but contemplative. It is not the result of any speculative reasoning or of understanding through experimental evidence, rather the flourishing of intuitive insight.

In the end, it isn't even a philosophy but a path that unfolds from within itself, reveals itself to itself. Even though it hides all our spiritual and enlightening potential in its embryo, the Path cannot blossom until we abandon the double-layered cocoon of illusion, woven from commonsensical faith in the sensory world and intellectual confidence in the world of abstract concepts.

VII.3 Wisdom is consciousness plus action

In the conscious man, there is not a moment's hesitation that would separate perception from action. Only such a man is truly alive and only such a man truly lives. The others who plan on bridling reality and organizing it in their rational frames not only miss out on reality, but also on their own lives.

Reason first tries to understand how to act, but this is a bad calculation. By the time it decides to take action, the circumstances have already changed and the original understanding is too late for reality, which is constantly moving and changing. Intellect, on the other hand, only requires the schemes and concepts according to which it can behave in, intercept and forestall reality, causing it to always remain one step behind reality.

Therefore, neither rationality nor intellectuality are nor can be wisdom. Wisdom comes from freedom, spontaneity, being integrated, from the ability to freely flow through confluence with reality, unbound to concepts. This, however, can only be achieved if you live in the presence.

However, being in the presence cannot be achieved by reading old writings and through intellectual musings such as "What is this supposed to mean?" Being in the presence may only be achieved through a systematic and disciplined practice of meditation such as used in Taoism and Zen Buddhism, in Tantra and Vedanta... In fact, here the doctrinal framework is in the background because the practice of presence is extremely simple, but before reaching that extreme simplicity the speculative mind needs to be outwitted for years, sometimes even decades.

When presence is cultivated through persistent discipline in such a way that it has practically become a second nature, then the conscious man can spontaneously respond to the sudden challenge of unforeseen circumstances with the entirety of his being, which is no longer divided into body and mind, reason and emotion, instinct and intellect. For lack of better words, we can say that man acts spontaneously and intuitively, even though intuition is only the sudden enlightenment of our true consciousness which is reflected currently and unannounced, while consciousness is the uninterrupted flow of that consciousness and its cognitive and active manifestation.

In the conscious man, there is not a moment's hesitation that would separate perception from action. Only such a man is truly alive and only such a man truly lives. The others who plan on bridling reality and organizing it in their rational frames not only miss out on reality, but also on their own lives.

VII.4 At the height of the search the seeker recognizes himself in the Sought after

This is a game that starts on its own when the Player wakes up from the deep silence of timeless oblivion and asks "Who am I?" A game that spontaneously stops when the Player, at the peak of the search for the depth that artists and mystics yearn for, once again meets himself, forgetting in that childlike playfulness about the One he had been searching for this whole time.

This whole universe with no beginning and no end is nothing but eternal Intelligence's self-expression. From the simplest forms of existence, that "big I", through all the more complex forms of existence, develops itself from the cocoon of unexpressed Being, questions itself, gets to know itself and tests all its resources. And through this incalculable, infinite imaginative creative play, this Intelligence feeds, outgrows, peels, transforms itself and at the end of it all returns to its confluence.

And every spark in this cosmic dance from which each individual temporal being is born is but the glistening top of the wave which scintillates only while its take-off lasts, in which all of existence is reflected, all of creation, as well as the mirroring images of a myriad of glittering waves, until it plunges back into the endless ocean.

Each spark is a piece of information about the Self, about the big Player who through the cosmic game expresses himself, gets to know himself, returns to himself. And so it goes over and over: giving birth to himself like a cosmic mother, he playing with himself like a curious child, collapsing into himself like a young man with Eros's lust and Ares's frenzy, returning to himself like a wilted old man longing for the calm of Hades.

This is a game that starts on its own when the Player wakes up from the deep silence of timeless oblivion and asks "Who am I?" A game that spontaneously stops when the Player, at the peak of the search for the depth that artists and mystics yearn for, once again meets himself, forgetting in that childlike playfulness about the One he had been searching for this whole time.

This is a game after which there will be nothing left to witness, nor anyone to witness; an endless wrinkling of time, a ripple of phenomena and space, a wave of existence... self--smitten absent Silence.

VII.5 The lens of the mutual mirroring of the internal and the external worlds

A free flux represents the immediacy of life, and resistance and control lead to death. He who does not experience this with his whole being remains bleeding in the painful jaws of the insidious paradox that is incomprehensible to reason: that our ego, antagonizing itself from the dynamic of the whole for the sake of its self-preservation, is slowly but surely, and in instalments, killing us.

The ego is the lens through which the inner and outer worlds mutually reflect themselves. As long as you reject the external world (or some of its aspects) with prejudices, the inner world that functions as its psychological negative will reject you in the same manner.

Similarly, like the reflection in a mirror, so long as you deny the reality of the inner, psychic world, the external world that acts like the objectification of our psychological projections will sabotage all your efforts to find harmony and balance in it.

Reject and you will be rejected. Accept and you will be accepted. Once you accept the external circumstances "as they are," your inner world begins to embrace and support you.

When you accept the internal dynamics of the psyche with benevolence, this outside world opens paths to you and becomes your guide to the heart of undivided existence.

When the outer and inner poles of unique existence become balanced, there is no longer a need for the ego, who divides the wholeness of life in order to control its changes, stubbornly resisting change and adaptation to its own identity.

The ego was created from resistance to the universal rhythm of change, because it sees the wholeness of existence as something different from itself and threatening to itself. However, when it realizes that that which it experiences in the external world is an unmistakable projection of the repressed contents of its unawakened inner world, and that the inner world continuously transforms itself through a series of reactions to the variable circumstances of the external world, then it understands that this unstoppable dynamic is the cause of its existence and that developing in accordance with it means accepting the natural flow and rhythm of change, rather than controlling and deadening it with abstract intellectual concepts.

For a free flux represents the immediacy of life, and resistance and control lead to death. He who does not experience this with his whole being remains bleeding in the painful jaws of the insidious paradox that is incomprehensible to reason: that our *ego*, antagonizing itself from the dynamic of the whole for the sake of its self-preservation, is slowly but surely and in instalments, killing us.

VII.6 Master of its own captivity

In saving its existence the ego does not understand that, from the Shadow of the unconscious field, it draws to the surface all the repressed, suppressed psychological states that will, once they have risen out into the light of consciousness, force it to transform. In other words, the ego, like any parasite, must continually adapt if it is to survive.

There is a higher will that exists in us, we could call it the longing for freedom, which seeks to liberate itself from the tyranny of the ego. But that chameleon, when it seems weakest to us, when it pretends to be near collapse, is actually preparing a devastating retaliation.

In order to survive, it has a whole hidden reservoir in the psyche's unconscious field available to it, from which, much in the same way a poisoned animal picks up the scent of a medicinal plant, it draws out all irrational forces and pitfalls, emotional games and manipulations with inconceivable precision. In short, an amazing combination of chess arsenal is at its disposition in order to defeat our longing for freedom and re-establish control, remaining the sole master of its own captivity.

At the same time, in saving its existence the ego does not understand that, from the Shadow of the unconscious field, it draws to the surface all the repressed, suppressed psychological states that will, once they have risen out into the light of consciousness, force it to transform. In other words, the ego, like any parasite, must continually adapt if it is to survive, and in doing so it cunningly uses the Shadow's inexhaustible mental resources.

But by drawing from it, it faces off with it and inevitably transforms. In order to be able to control and channel them, it is forced to change its defensive formation because if it wants to survive a meeting with them, it cannot remain the same. Although its instinct for self-preservation, as the underlying motive that sets it in motion, is ready to destroy our psycho-physical individuum if this is necessary to its survival, it actually totally unconsciously and indirectly allows a gradual reintegration of the psyche's unconscious contents into the field of consciousness, and thus inadvertently enables the progressive expansion of our consciousness.

And so its fundamental imperative "Adapt to survive!" indirectly enables the integration and development of our consciousness. But when it finds itself in a double trap between the psychological Shadow's instinctive demands and the higher will's demand for freedom, whether it wants to or not, it must cede control to the being's spiritual center, our authentic I, in order to complete the mental integration and to return to our being its lost unity with the spiritual Source.

But if the ego refuses to relinquish control until the last moment, it will be taken from him by force by an invasion of unconscious forces, and then instead of spiritual reintegration, what usually arises is psychic regression in the form of a variety of disorders, such as deep neurosis, depression, psychosis and severe splits in the personality.

VII.7 The struggle of our lives – the battle against the Grand Inquisitor in us

It is only when we learn how to live while abandoning all images and qualifications of our selves that the Judge will no longer have anyone to judge. And then, between these two phantoms, that of the inquisitor and the heretic, there will not even be a split the size of a needle's eye.

The battle against the discriminatory mind or Judge Within Us is in fact the central, if not the only true battle in our lives. It's a battle to the death, a battle with the master of our desire and hate, our hopes and disappointments, with the way we live and ultimately die.

For the Judge has the power to make us in his own image if we obey him or to break us, cripple us (first morally and mentally through constant blackmail, underestimation and condemnation, manipulation and imputation, a devastating feeling of guilt, and then physically through diseases such as the flip side to internal self-destruction) and ultimately kill us, if we try to resist him.

All teachings, ideologies and religions support that Grand Inquisitor, and worship him like an irreplaceable idol. All that the human mind can understand serves this idol, to strengthen him. All that we seem to have discovered, learned, come to know, he claims and thus additionally confirms and supports himself. With all this fake or so-called knowledge, he builds and tears down, rises again from the debris, grinds and recycles this magnificent image of the world and of the builder, and stands himself in the middle of that impenetrable labyrinth built of sheer fantasy.

That is why his virtual network cannot be escaped by anyone who hasn't yet understood that they could renounce their little, selfish ego. He who, with all that he does, only maintains his own image continues to spin in a spiral of self-delusion. Since our egoism feeds the Inquisitor, the only path by which we can escape his tyranny is the Path of self-forgetfulness through the knowledge of our true I.

It is only when we learn how to live while abandoning all images and qualifications of our selves that the Judge will no longer have anyone to judge. And then, between these two phantoms, that of the inquisitor and the heretic, there will not even be a split the size of a needle's eye.

After it all the phantoms of night delirium can quietly melt, like the morning mist before the self-awakening, radiating sun of the great Awakening.

VIII. AN EMPTY COCOON
FROM THE START

In order to break out of a prison, one first must confess to being in a prison. The trap is man's emotional structure, his character structure. There is little use in devising systems of thought about the nature of the trap if the only thing to do in order to get out of the trap is to know the trap and to find the exit.

Wilhelm Reich, psychoanalysis's most radical

outcast and the author of the original character analysis

Transitoriness is depressing only to the mind which insists upon trying to grasp. But to the mind which lets go and moves with the flow of change, which becomes, in Zen Buddhist imagery, like a ball in a mountain stream, the sense of transience or emptiness becomes a kind of ecstasy.

Alan Watts: The Way of Zen

VIII.1 Where there isn't room for two

The self-love is born of limited ego; self-will is born of self-love, and selfishness of self-will. This is the Holy Trinity of the deluded son who has lost consciousness of his Primary Nature. These three are the uterus which gives birth to the suffering of human limitation, alienation and lack of self-sufficiency, the suffering whose source and causes we most often search for in the world, and almost never in ourselves.

Consciously and willfully surrendering to one's Authentic Nature or Self is the shortest path to liberation. For he who consciously surrenders to his Self frees himself of the coercion of an unwilling subjugation to the ego's tyranny.

As the Self is the real center and the totality of our existence until he turns to It in his vain quest for a base, both in the external world of objects and in the inner world of subjective concepts, man cannot get out of his ego's dungeon-like circle.

Not a single being in creation can find freedom until it turns its attention and will towards its center, the center which is the origin of our consciousness, will and life. As long as our attention and will, and thus life force, are turned towards our pseudo-center, man instinctively is subjugated to the tyranny of the limited ego.

The self-love is born of limited ego; self-will is born of self--love, and selfishness of self-will. This is the Holy Trinity of the deluded son who has lost consciousness of his Primary Nature. These three are the uterus which gives birth to the suffering of human limitation, alienation and lack of self-sufficiency, the suffering whose source and causes we most often search for in the world, and almost never in ourselves. It is only when we see through the depth of the self-delusion in ourselves that we will be capable of relinquishing self-love and surrendering ourselves to our True Being; just to realize at the height of this devotion that in it, there isn't room for two.

On the other hand, all while the ego is his center, man can travel across the whole world without ever crossing his own threshold. But when the Self becomes his life's axis, without even leaving his home man can visit countless hearts because the Self resides in the niche of everyone's heart. Until he awakens his Self as his life's axis, man will wrestle with the ego's tyranny, seeking a vent for it through escapes into various forms of self-oblivion (emotionless promiscuous adventures, hazardous and other various aggressive games) and neurotic passion, unaware that in doing so he is establishing new forms of tyranny over himself.

Through neurotic repetition these short-lived escapes are perverted into sick addictions and competing ambitions that lead to egocentric self-affirmation and do not bring lasting fulfillment, instead leaving an emptiness in the soul that was ravaged by narcissistic self-destruction.

However, when with the power of consciousness, which releases an obstructed will, he turns his attention from an obsession with himself and directs it with his whole being toward the Self as his spiritual source, man frees himself of the penitential burden that is his ego and finds freedom in self-forgetfulness.

VIII.2 Being one's own labyrinth and door to freedom

Only few, when they find the traces of those who have managed to escape, reject all stale theories and concepts and without hesitation follow in their footsteps towards an exit. For when they realize that they are themselves their own labyrinth and their own door, any further delay becomes superfluous. Who is still standing at the threshold of his own home and asks: Is there anyone inside? Who is still waiting instead of stepping through an open door?

Man is born, lives, wanders and dies in the labyrinth of his own delusions, self-delusions and obsessions with himself. What can really be important to him who was sentenced to starve in the underground catacombs of his unconsciousness or to be devoured by the Minotaur of his own hopelessness, in the unlikelihood that he will ever find a way out of the labyrinth?

People spend most of their time on nonsense such as how to engineer an escape from the labyrinth, or on how to draw a map that will allow sovereign movement throughout the labyrinth, as well as on the study of the life, character and works of greats who, wandering through these tunnels, have created epochal works and made tremendous cultural and scientific achievements. Most of these people, though, have never actually found a way out of the labyrinth, much like the average cleaner of the dark and distressing tunnels of the unawakened pole of the mental being.

Some, therefore, merely make plans for an escape to freedom, which for them is a pure category of the imagination. Others simply study the works of great *sleep walkers* who have raised magnificent monuments for their own somnambulism (the greater the delusion, the bigger the monuments). Still others do not even seek an exit but look to dominate the labyrinth, to establish a party and appoint themselves as the *great leader* or to enthrone themselves as the *main procurer* and force others to prostitute themselves for them.

But these are all short-range strategies, strategies that are not focused on achieving personal freedom but that merely adapt and pander to the most mundane survival instincts. Few dare to move towards the exit because fear makes the darkness even more opaque, and the Minotaur appears to be omnipresent and to lurk behind every door that offers hope of a *break towards freedom.*

Only few, when they find the traces of those who have managed to escape, reject all stale theories and concepts and without hesitation follow in their footsteps towards an exit. For when they realize that they are themselves their own labyrinth and their own door, any further delay becomes superfluous.

Who still supports their own mask and tries to emulate Theseus instead of waking his slumbering *Self*? Who still allows their own mental Shadow to pull them by the tip of their nose, whispering: *Bow down to me, you are but a shadow*! Who is still standing at the threshold of his own home and asks: *Is there anyone inside*? Who is still waiting instead of stepping through an open door? Who is still dreaming of a victory over the Minotaur, of love with Ariadne and of the Minos's crown, not realizing that he is sleeping like the dead in a prepared coffin, just waiting for someone to bury him?

But there are also those who think that the maze is located outside them, that is, that all the problems that they face come from the outside, from the world and from others, and that the Minotaur (their unconscious *ego* that is conditioned by instincts and affects) can be kept at a respectful distance and restrained with the offer of an occasional *sacrifice,* and these are usually compromises of all kinds whose goals are to avoid confrontation with the unawakened part of their being. However, such compromises are barren, and in the long run lead to a regression which could result in different types of communication and mental health problems.

Given the way our unconscious field binds huge reserves of psychic energy without which no man has the will or strength to resist instinctive compulsion and dependencies, it is not surprising that such inert *aristocrats* lease a professional (Theseus in the demanding and ungrateful role of the psychotherapist, guru or exorcist to our intimate demons) to solve their personal problems for them.

But Theseus, who is much more than that (above all, he is the archetype of the internal pathfinder-warrior who fearlessly confronts man's lowly *ego*) will show them the grotesqueness of their conceit and the depth of their unconsciousness: that they are no masters of the labyrinth, but slaves of their own delusion.

And what then can be more valuable to all those *slumbering fools*: To continue blissfully dreaming or to simply, no matter how uncomfortable it be, wake up?

VIII.3 A quantum leap from a regulated to an unpredictable regime

The instant falling of the veil can be described as a sudden transition from a regulated state that our ego attempts to control as an external controller, to the original state of natural unpredictability that is beyond any possibility of control. In it everything is in original harmony with everything else, precisely because there is no more separate controller that could disrupt this natural harmony by imposing artificial regulations.

Memory that shapes the *image of the I* is not the True Self. It's only the ego's hardened, lifeless structure, whose primary motive is to create the kind of psychological self-organization which enables the most reliable self-preservation mechanism with minimum power consumption.

Such an organization does not favor the self-development of individuality; it is there to protect the ego from the uncertain trials of life, hence the mental energy in such a rigid structure is unable to *flow* naturally, adjusting itself to the spontaneous and dynamic changes in life. But memory is also a pledge of individualization, the separation of the personal *ego* from undifferentiated collective consciousness, species instinct and tribal atavisms. Were man not to have the ability to remember, he would not be able to differentiate and form his own individual *ego*.

On the other hand, thanks to that, the formation, organization, and existence of the ego-complex is like a dream. Because he lives in the memories of the past and in the images of the future, but it never lives the only possible authentic life, the one *here and now*.

That is why liberation or awakening from a dream into real life is only possible through the *ego's self-forgetfulness*, the self--forgetfulness that can occur during the process of deep meditation on the true nature of our I (where *the I that meditates* vanishes like the self-grasping hand). Or through unconditional surrender to one's true being, the *Self* (where *the I that surrenders* melts into that devotion like an anchor made of salt that measures the depths of the ocean).

Even a brief moment of awakening is enough to realize that ego is nothing more than *its own dream*. From step to step, breath to breath we move through our own consciousness's space, still not aware of the dream that we dream. For the moment that we become aware of it, the dream would dissolve, and we would become *Awakened*.

The following question is therefore posited to the careful observer: *How is it possible, for the Self and the dream, for consciousness and visions from dreams to simultaneously exist?* This is the secret that has only been unveiled by the *awakened*. This is the veil that everyone must lift from their *spiritual eye*, from their *internal mirror*.

The instant falling of the veil can be described as a sudden transition from a regulated state that our *ego* attempts to control as an external controller, to the original state of natural unpredictability that is beyond any possibility of control. Still, this state cannot be described as chaotic. On the contrary, in it everything is in original harmony with everything else, precisely because there is no more separate controller that could disrupt this natural harmony by imposing artificial regulations.

For it is not the material world that is the weave which binds us and keeps us caught up in deception; the threads that that support the veil of illusion are figments of our imagination and our dreams' illusions. It is not hard to renounce the world; but it is difficult to give up our dreams, those ghosts that feed our ego. Why then should we renounce the valuable opportunities that the world gives us to understand the illusiveness of our notions of ourselves and of the world?

We dream because we are afraid of reality, because we cannot withstand the pressure of reality. But if Reality has always been one, unique and indivisible, how has this contagious, moldy, deadened dream crawled into it like a worm, formed around it like a cobweb?

This game of creation and self oblivion, of searching for and re-remembering our True Nature, is a game that never ends. Becoming conscious, waking up and emerging from our dreams while accepting the naked Reality without any conditions or reservations is the only profit that this timeless game gives us.

VIII.4 The mind is the architect of all divides and the border it creates in the process

Although the mind is continuously experiencing pain because of its separation from True Nature, due to this separation it is unable to understand the causes of its suffering. It therefore tries to keep the pain under control, tries to keep the states and circumstances that it detects as the source of its suffering at arm's length, it even tries to create a defense structure that would make it invulnerable, but in fact it really only provides a short-term illusion of untouchability.

As we said, the discriminatory mind is the one which divides the psyche's and life's original unity into conscious and unconscious, spirit and matter, internal and external, rational and irrational, etc. and a multitude of other categories and divisions, all with the intention of trying to control the unruly world of phenomena, whose interdependence and volatility it does not understand, by dividing it into rational categories and neatly putting it away in intellectual drawers, like any good registrar.

But in nature there is no such registry and dead system of categories. That is why man's True Nature revolts against all the divisions that come from the mind; because it recognizes that the mind cannot understand the primordial *unity of nature*, since the mind's conditional nature is: endless divisions and boundaries, control, authority and power, rule, judgment and punishment, etc. for the path of division has no end.

Although the mind is continuously experiencing pain because of its separation from True Nature, due to this separation it is unable to understand the causes of its suffering. It therefore tries to keep the pain under control, tries to keep the states and circumstances that it detects as the *source of its suffering* at arm's length, it even tries to create a defense structure that would make it *invulnerable*, but in fact it really only provides a short-term illusion of untouchability. Unfortunately, the initial failures will not hinder the mind in the development of complex psychological defense mechanisms until it sees that its suffering does not come from the outside (from the objective world of phenomena), but from its separation from the Source.

On the other hand, the True Nature is never divided (i. e. it never goes through the illusion of the separation of Consciousness from its states) and therefore it cannot be said that it really suffers due to division or that it resists the minds dividing activities. It is, as the Vedas and Upanishads beautifully interpret it, the infinite *Existence-Consciousness-Bliss* that is beyond all objective differentiation and subjective discrimination.

If it really is as such, then we must ask ourselves the following questions: *Who is it that suffers? Who resists the divides? Who seeks to be freed of the constant slavery of discrimination?* It is the mind that in its ignorance and separation divides, oppresses and enslaves itself!

But at the bottom of its vortex, at the center of its blind natural element, in the heart of the continuously streaming current, sooner or later it must find the inexhaustible, lively, constantly flowing Spring of its dynamics. This spring is the source of all beings and creations that were created by the mind, and in creating them it ostensibly divided itself into countless phenomena.

In the end, this spring is the mind's very Source, as well as the source of its incurable longing for a return to its *original unity*. This is precisely why the mind cannot put an end to its endless spinning until it returns to the source and dissolves in it, like an anchor made of salt trying to measure its depth.

VIII.5 The Self and the ego or the Prince and the pauper

Therefore the ego suffers, caught between two traps: the desire for self-preservation that it binds itself with and the desire for freedom that leads him to the brink of self-annihilation. Just like the mind cannot destroy itself by force, the ego cannot attain self-forgetfulness, i. e. take the leap into the abyss of self-

-transcendence, until it has matured within and its fundamental origin is reflected, and that is the Core of self-knowledge.

Modern self-knowledge teachings don't successfully harmonize traditions from Eastern spiritual disciplines such as Vedanta and Yoga, Tantra and Zen with a variety of Western psychological doctrines from scientific psychology. More often than not, this causes the seeker to feel more confusion than clarity.

This is why, for example, some modern teachers say that the greatest obstacle to human freedom is the mind, and that the mind should be controlled, subjugated, annihilated. We have a few complaints in regards to such teachings.

First, it is impossible to control the mind without understanding what it is and its function within man's mental and physical constitution. Second, violent attempts to annihilate the mind can only create even deeper psychological divides and problems. The mind itself is not a problem; the problem is in how it is used. This is why first it is important to understand how the mind works.

And so, first we must become aware of the fact that the mind is nothing more than universal Consciousness's creative force (chitishakti) which is manifested in each individual being as its instinctive, driving will. Acting naturally (unconsciously at first) through a single form, the mind does nothing other than spontaneously try to return to the Source it originated from. However, since it lost its original unconditioned consciousness in an individual form, it acts overshadowed by individual consciousness, conditioned by senses and impressions.

Acting through an individual form, the mind manifests four basic functions: remembering, storing and expressing impressions, differentiating and distributing impressions, and identifying with the individual form, and thus forming the being's individual center. As was said in previous chapters, this *pseudo-center* is but a *prosthetic limb* with which we attempt to compensate for our true center or our Self.

As we can see, the mind does nothing but seek a way back to its source, unaware that it is merely the original unconditioned Consciousness's function or active force. However, the mind that is conditioned and divided into functions becomes weakened and disintegrated. This blind force that has no leadership becomes disoriented, and the ego takes it upon itself to assume the function of guide. From that moment onwards, it is the ego that accumulates, draws, manipulates and mobilizes with the mind's power for one purpose only, its self-preservation.

But the ego is nothing but a pauper who has sat on the Prince's throne. Moreover, it is a blind pauper that leads a blind mind, and we all know how it ends when the blind lead the blind. Since the underlying motive that drives the ego is its self-preservation, it constantly keeps the mind divided because the reunion of mind and Self would abolish the ego's existence, it would remove the pauper from the throne and return the Prince on it. (Although, truth be told, the Prince had never descended from his throne, he had only dreamt a bittersweet dream about his abdication and wanderings in the rags of a pauper).

Therefore the ego suffers, caught between two traps: the desire for self-preservation that it binds itself with and the desire for freedom that leads him to the brink of self-annihilation. Just like the mind cannot destroy itself by force, the ego cannot attain self-forgetfulness, i. e. take the leap into the abyss of self--transcendence, until it has matured within and its fundamental origin is reflected, and that is the *Core of self-knowledge.*

Metaphorically speaking, when the Prince wakes up, the pauper along with his rags will disappear like a dream. When the *Core* is released and actualized, that very moment our consciousness becomes aware of the ego's ostensibility. Then the *mind's river* naturally returns to the source of its efflux; without violence and suffering, with the strength of pure self-awakening.

VIII.6 An empty cocoon from the start

Despite the convincing arguments provided by our senses, reason and intellect, that cocoon is only a dream that will vanish one day, showing that a larvae never existed in it, and neither did the possibility of emerging from that cocoon as a butterfly. Whether it was a mere illusion or simply a metaphor, one thing is for certain, and that is that the cocoon was empty from the very start.

What is it that separates the unitary Being into a divided ego, into an entire legion of "psychological tenants"? This is the question of all questions, for without it there is no confinement, no Path, no liberation.

As soon as the un-displayed One manifests itself as the universe and uncountable multitude of individual beings (jiva), in each of these beings the One remains the center of its organization and existence, in the same way that it remains the organization and maintenance center of all of creation. However, to the individual being that is misguided by the world of countless phenomena and forms that One or absolute Self (Brahman) is manifested as a distorted reflection in a broken mirror, as a so-called false ego (ahamkara). That is why mystics say that the created world is like a mirror that reflects God's numerous attributes, but cannot reflect God's pure essence, which can only be reflected in the mystic's purified heart.

And this false reflection, this mere echo of the primordial vibration which is the foundation of the entire manifest reality is accepted by the being as its ego, as the center of its being and self-awareness, forgetting the Source from which the echo started and the way in which the illusion was manifested.

Until the mirror of our consciousness is completely free of adhering to the world of phenomena and forms, we will not be able to fully and clearly see through the illusion; through the way in which the true Self (reflected by the appearance of this world, the illusion that is created by the reciprocal relationship of objectified phenomena, by the senses of the subject who observes and by the deluded mind that conceived them) is displayed as our small, conditioned ego.

Since this false reflection, this image of the ego is the basis of the misleading conceptions we have of creation and existence and our place in it, out of love for preserving these images and ideas the false ego isolates itself as an autonomous entity, separated from the rest of existence. And so begins the endless division, fragmentation and segregation of the mind from the forms that it creates, of Intelligence from its creations, of the ego from the other, of Consciousness from its states and contents...

What remains in this endless dividing? The pure virtual projection of our unconscious aspirations and needs. The lie of all lies. The great illusion of religions, philosophies, psychologies... For that One, what the ultimate Reality is, what the Being is, what the universe is, has always been whole and undivided. And since It is entire in Itself, there is no center around which to revolve, no limits to be surpassed.

For those who are capable of living, moving, being, flowing without a center like a river – creating, traveling, imprisonment and release is but a playful illusion. For when it exists without a center, for the being there are neither boundaries nor divides between it and others, between creation and the creative Spirit.

The body is not a boundary because the True Being's body is the entire universe. The walls that separate us from other creatures are not outside us, but within us. And as long as we believe that these walls are real, as long as we believe that through a separate existence we are separated from everything else, we will need the protective cocoon, our false ego.

However, despite the convincing arguments provided by our senses, reason and intellect, that cocoon is only a dream that will vanish one day, showing that a larvae never existed in it, and neither did the possibility of emerging from that cocoon as a butterfly.

Whether it was a mere illusion or simply a metaphor, one thing is for certain, and that is that the cocoon was empty from the very start.

VIII.7 Creativity and contemplation arise from an intelligent space

Such a space, whether internal or external, frees with its insatiability the possibility that in it, consciousness's True Nature can be momentarily reflected; this Nature standing in the background of all phenomena and vibrating in the heart of all forms, no matter how transient and unstable they be.

How we handle the area around and inside us is crucial to the path of establishing harmony between consciousness and space. Namely, the way we deal with the space around us indicates how we deal with our inner space.

A space cluttered with objects or thoughts is a cramped, congested, undynamic, inoperable space. A space that is freed of spare objects or mental contents is free, playful, creative, surprising. This is a space which constantly gives birth to energy and contemplation, creation and poetry out of its emptiness... This is an intelligently used space. Moreover, it is an *intelligent space.*

The poetics and aesthetics of Zen art simply and impressively confirm this. The Zen gardening artist does not need a large space in order to, with a couple of rocks, a pile of gravel or sand, the occasional bush or a moss buildup that are seemingly loosely *scattered* everywhere, express *Nature's* integrity, its lively dynamism, as well as the universe's basic principles at the same time.

The same goes for the Sumi-e painter who with a few ink stains and a couple of quick, sharp strokes with a brush can sum up in one scene, which is dominated by the white freshness of empty space, the creative originality of life that we express in our every action, gesture, move. We become all the more inexhaustible in our creative liberation the deeper we are immersed in the Path which we have never treaded nor will we ever complete.

Such a space, whether internal or external, frees with its insatiability the possibility that in it, consciousness's True Nature can be momentarily reflected; this Nature standing in the background of all phenomena and vibrating in the heart of all forms, no matter how transient and unstable they be.

The sameness and simultaneity of this vibration/reflection from which springs the creative and cognitive potential of human beings is possible thanks to the natural harmony of mind and space that should be cultivated in two ways:

a. through sitting meditation (e. g. Zen meditation known as zazen)

b. through meditation in motion (e. g., painting, gardening or exercises such as tai chi chuan).

Through the systematic practice of such meditation we can directly experience that space and time come from the mind (here we refer to the universal Mind that is specifically expressed through all phenomena and all living beings, that most beings are not aware of) and that the mind is nothing but omnipresent Consciousness's vibration which expands through all these phenomena and, through the reflection in manifested objects, once again gathers itself in the Primal Point, the center and the source of the universe that is woven of phenomena and their names.

IX. WHO IS IT THAT HARNESSES US IN ITS PLOUGH SO THAT WE TILL THE LAND OF ITS ILLUSIONS

The mind builds a tower of thoughts and then gets entangled in them. And so it creates its own suffering and experiences the consequences... The mind can never be satisfied, it will always create a handful of desires.

Swami Muktananda,

founder of the Siddha Yoga

Yet this consideration is the only one that can permanently console us, when, on the one hand, we have recognized incurable suffering and endless misery as essentially linked to the phenomenon of the will, to the world, and on the other see the world melt away with the abolished will, and retain before us only empty nothingness.

Arthur Schopenhauer:

The World as Will and Representation

IX.1 *Spare parts* have no individuality or autonomy

Society does not need us as confident individuals, because in the depths of our (un)consciousness, everyone knows that the individual is irreplaceable. Society needs us as solidly tuned and refined, flexible and adaptable spare parts in a well-oiled social mechanism, because spare parts have no individuality or autonomy.

The authentic personal Path begins when we take responsibility for our actions and for our own lives. Of all the duties we assume throughout our lives, towards our family, neighbors, community, etc., the greatest one we have is towards ourselves. And that means being willing to live without compromising what we really are. Without taking these responsibilities, we cannot honestly take on any other duties, nor can we commit to them, nor are we worthy of carrying them out...

If we are not honest with ourselves, who can we be honest with? If we deceive ourselves, we will deceive the whole world. If we do not believe in ourselves and we do not love ourselves, who can we believe, who can we love sincerely? Jesus says, "Love thy neighbor as yourself!" But as long as we do not fully accept and love ourselves, with all our imperfections and immaturity, who we can fully accept and love?

Therefore, sincere actions can come only from a sincere heart which lives according to its own moral criteria and not according to socially constructed criteria; and this is called moral autonomy and personal integrity. The first step towards moral autonomy and personal integrity is taking responsibility for our own actions. Who does not dare to do so, regardless of the price to pay, will wander in the maze of rotten compromises and in the end despise himself, that conformist and compromising self.

We cannot expect others to provide us with what we refuse or do not dare to give ourselves. We cannot expect honesty and responsibility, authenticity, respect and love in relationships with others if we do not offer ourselves the same. Society does not raise us for this; society does not teach us to be authentic, morally independent people of integrity. It trains us to be flexible and useful, usable and obedient, in short, people without a backbone or personal identity.

Society does not need us as confident individuals, because in the depths of our (un)consciousness, everyone knows that the individual is irreplaceable. Society needs us as solidly tuned and refined, flexible and adaptable spare parts in a well-oiled social mechanism, because *spare parts* have no individuality or autonomy. Their value is measured by how useful they are within the mechanism. That is why from a very early age, such *individuals with no integrity* are raised to believe that they are worthless outside the social mechanism. And anyone who accepts this almost certainly has no hope of further personal development.

Society has been doing this to the individual since the beginning of time; from tribal times to Antiquity, to feudal times all the way to civil society it has repeated the same game of social manipulation. For society does not need a liberated individual. He does not fit into any of the structures that society has to offer. To any society, the liberated man is a heretic, a subversive, a renegade.

Ultimately, society does not need any kind of individual in terms of a psychological autonomous individual, but it does need biological entities: sawed-off, trimmed and numbered like socio-culturally unified logs, which may be sent where needed, to do what is needed and, with no qualms whatsoever, be dumped in the trash and indifferently replaced, just like all worn-out inventory.

All this is possible precisely because society has no moral autonomy or unique integrity. Society is an *amorphous mechanism* with no true identity which, as such, is supported by the rulers and political elites because this Moloch, to whom they ritually sacrifice legions of blind followers, crucifying any individual that dares to point out that monstrous mechanism's Pharisaic deformation, is the only guarantee of their parasitic existence.

Such a society is not a society of free individuals, such a society (be it secular or religious, ideological or vocational) is an organization centered around the cult dedicated to the self-preservation of one's own parasitic organism and not to the betterment and development of each individual or to the support of one's development into a free and independent individual.

History has proved that all such societies must change or collapse since they are built from the very start on rotten value systems. No matter how powerful and ornate they were from the outside, all systems that were built on the rotten pillars of manipulation, repression and exploitation, eventually sank into a pestilent bog, blossomed within their own ruin.

The Western Roman Empire lasted 1300 years; the Eastern Roman Empire or Byzantium lasted 1000 years. They were probably the longest-running empires of our civilization, and both ultimately failed because in their bellies, no matter how much they spread outwardly, both empires nurtured the demon of their own corruption and self-destruction; the only real Moloch which eventually brings every worshiper, be it an individual or a system, to their demise.

And so it is with every organism: biological, social, psychological, which, in order to survive, follows the path of rotten compromises and not the path of its own authenticity. Jesus said: "For what doth it profit a man, if he gain the whole world, and suffer the loss of his own soul?" He knew well that only a city built on solid rock can withstand any storm and that the facades of "whitewashed tombs" will eventually be denuded and show its malformed inner self in the light of day.

Time is the strongest guarantor or subversive of any kind of learning, as of this one. All systems that are based on lies and manipulation were unmasked by history and dissolved like rotting corpses in acid. But the individual's indestructible gait to his own authenticity and freedom has lasted since the beginning of time and will continue to last forever; no history and no one's history will ever be able to cover that path's tracks.

IX.2 The world is a marketplace and the ego a never satisfied merchant in it

Whether it is an adventurer chasing the wind, a romantic fool or a bookworm, every ego at the end of its' life journey will admit that it is unfulfilled, unfinished and disappointed... because up until the very last moment, the ego is incapable of seeing that it is behaving like a dog furiously chasing its own tail.

Sigmund Freud, the father of psychoanalysis and founder of *ego psychology*, once wrote that the ego's life is really pathetic because it has to trade with the id and with the super-ego, as well as with the outer and its inner world, all in order to survive.

Although he was right in terms of the ego's position, Freud unfortunately never took it further than that because he never recognized the existence of a deeper I or Self. Freud's associate who later became the most famous renegade of classical psychoanalysis, Swiss psychologist Carl Gustav Jung, was the first modern Western psychologist to identify the true center of our psychological integrity or Self.

But let's set aside the paths and side-tracks of the hundred-year-old development of psychoanalysis and go directly to the question that any sincere seeker on the Path of Self-Knowledge is most intimately interested in, and that question goes as follows: Why can our life, under the ego's guidance, never completely be fulfilled or satisfied? Based on personal experience, the answer is brief and clear: *because such a life is barren spinning around in circles.*

We must get off the *wheel* (as Buddhists and Hindus would claim, referring to the "samsara's wheel") or the unconscious existence conditioned by the mechanical law of cause and effect. We must get out of this arid and uncreative circle; we must relieve ourselves of the great "market of vanity's" criteria and nexus, but we can only do this when we allow the reins of our lives to be taken into the Self's hands.

Whether it is an adventurer chasing the wind (a man of action who acts first and considers the consequences later), a romantic fool (a Werther who wanders in the impenetrable fog of illusory sentiments), or a bookworm (a marble statue at a podium on which only the *Adam's apple* is real), every ego at the end of its' life journey will admit that it is unfulfilled, unfinished and disappointed... because up until the very last moment, the ego is incapable of seeing that it is behaving like a dog furiously chasing its own tail.

In this context, bargainers and anyone "who plays safe", anyone who hides behind social institutions and collective structures will have difficulties persevering on this Path. Only seekers who are able to leave their own footprints behind, who are able to leave the temporary shelter they have built and even more quickly leave behind the lodgings that others have constructed for them, only seekers who are able to leave all fixed games and learned steps and who free of any baggage can release themselves into the *Unknown* can dare to take the Path of Self-Knowledge.

Only such a Path leads to freedom; everything else leads to being a lifelong slave to a false sense of security.

IX.3 Neither from the outside nor from the inside, or the *middle path* to balance

The East is introverted, the West is extroverted. However, regardless of tradition, most search for their center of gravity in someone or something else: in social or religious institutions, in work or family, in career or partners. However, a stable balance can only be found in the Self. It is a calling which existence sends to every individual.

Everything in the universe, including man, strives to reach its optimal balance. Some physicists, based on the second law of thermodynamics (which states that in an energetically isolated system, all differences in temperature spontaneously seek to cancel each other out) predict that a heat death of the universe is inevitable (provided that the universe is an energetically closed system and not a network of open systems).

Modern science's predictions are partly confirmed by the ancient spiritual teachings such as the oldest Hindu philosophical school, *Samkhya*, which says something similar about that issue. According to this doctrine, when it comes to the perfect balance between the three cosmic principles (Gunas) – movement (Rajas), inertia (Tamas) and harmony (Sattva), all of creation will be withdrawn into its original latency (pralaya) or into a state of non-manifestation.

Since man's psychophysical system also naturally strives to establish and maintain an optimal balance, it is reasonable to assume that our personal growth and spiritual development is the all the more conscious expression of this unconscious biological principle. In light of this, it is interesting to note how Zen Buddhists point out that this balance in our consciousness arises when the mind's constant movement ceases, whether towards the inside or the outside. Then the *self-adhesive mind* is ripe to fall off, and the Buddha nature is free to dawn.

The enlightenment experience described by Japanese Zen master Sokei-an Shigetsu Sasaki (1882-1945) is very well illustrated: "One day I wiped out all the notions from my mind. I gave up all desire. I discarded all the words with which I thought and stayed in quietude. I felt a little queer – as if I were being carried into something, or as if I were touching some power unknown to me... and Ztt! I lost the boundary of my physical body. (...) I had believed that I was created, but now I must change my opinion: I was never created; I was the cosmos; no individual Mr. Sasaki existed."

Eccentric Chinese Zen master Lin Chi spoke of this in a unique, metaphorical way, saying "I standing here respect neither monks nor laymen," monks symbolically representing *introverts* whose mind constantly wanders in the interior spaces of the subjective world, and laymen representing *extroverts* whose mind is constantly chasing objects belonging to the external world.

However, despite the clarity and logic of these concepts, such highly balanced individuals are extremely a rare phenomenon; for the balance of instincts which are under the pressure of the principle of Tamas, the affects that are under the control of the principle of Rajas, and reason guided by the principle of Sattva (which each in their own way try to appropriate *consciousness's energy* and so constantly encourage unrest and the mind's wandering) is not achieved in one lifetime. It takes many lives to develop all the layers of our being uniformly and for our consciousness to stabilize itself during its self-development in the center of this balance, which we will call Heart (Hridaya).

The East is introverted, the West is extroverted. However, regardless of tradition, most search for their center of gravity in someone or something else: in social or religious institutions, in work or family, in career or partners. However, a stable balance can only be found in the Self. It is a calling which existence sends to every individual.

For it is necessary to first find balance in oneself in order to achieve a balance with the community and with nature. The West has seriously perturbed all levels (psychological, social, environmental) of man's balance because it has given priority to will and intellect over the heart, in accordance with the typical pragmatic Western principle "Seek and Destroy!".

This causes us to forget the ancient wisdom that teaches us that the *Heart* is the center of our balance. When it is neglected, closed and "in hibernation," all kinds of imbalances are developed: psycho-physical and social, moral and spiritual.

The Path to Self-Knowledge is the most natural and most direct way to restore this lost balance through:

a. the internal understanding of the complementarity of mind and body, consciousness and the world,

b. centering in the Heart of balance through meditation,

c. surrendering to our True Self through devotion and contemplation.

It is impossible to put in words how important the systematic cultivation and development of a balanced person is for the individual, for society and for nature. For example let's start from the phenomenon that is closest to us, the family.

To the enlightened person that is freed of tribal prejudices and the superstitious dogmas of primitive environments on the one side, and the arrogant ignorance that in mega-urban modern society gives birth to an alienated *asphalt jungle* on the other, it is not necessary to explain that it is only when two balanced beings meet that a true relationship, a partnership, a life and marital relationship can blossom, out of which a balanced descendants can develop and be raised. However, since most individuals are unevenly developed, unbalanced, rather neurotic, each of these individuals, through the infallible neurotic mechanism of compensation, seeks in the other its still unawakened opposite, or, simply put, it seeks what it lacks.

And when the individual finds it, he then shows (surprisingly!) that he really does not want to accept the opposite quality in his partner. Rather, he wants to impose himself on, to incorporate his partner into his own socio-psychological organization, through which he tries to adapt life to himself instead of adapting to life. It is paradoxical but true that he ego always identifies with its dominant quality, whether it be rationality, emotivity or instinctivity, while it considers the other repressed, undeveloped or unawakened qualities inferior, both when displayed in himself and in others.

It is not strange that almost every *ego* tries to impose its dominant quality onto its partner that has opposite qualities (and opposites, as everything in nature shows us, are strongly attracted but hardly ever in harmony with each other) and adapt its partner to its own vision and organization of life. Of course, since each ego defends his position to the death because he neither knows nor understands a different life strategy, this is how what is popularly called the *war of the sexes* begins, though it is in fact a *war of egos*.

Neurotic relationship are developed from such starting positions, neurotic families from such relationships, such families develop neurotic descendants that keep spinning in that vicious neurotic circle, in which most of the human population on this planet unconsciously and helplessly spin.

How can we get out of this circle? The bad news is that there is no collective exit. The good news is that only the Path to Self-Knowledge on which each of us is called can bring us to the exit. All we need to do is start off...

IX.4 Who is it that harnesses us in its plough so that we till the land of its illusions?

A freeing consciousness is available to everyone because it is in all of us; moreover, we swim in it like fish in water. Still, we are entertained by the waste that waves have brought out to the coast beyond the ocean of spiritual Consciousness in us. We are trained like seagulls, we rummage through mental garbage and we satisfy our hunger with carcasses instead of discovering the wealth of spiritual life within ourselves.

We have everything in ourselves from birth: the ability to create, know, love, admire, wonder... We are endowed with everything that can make us happy, without the soul-caring intervention from the outside, everything that can guide us on our way, which can help us to develop and finally break free. In nature, we can find everything we need for a simple, modest and balanced life that is enough for us to devote ourselves to self-realization and self-development.

Still, from an early age we are taught the opposite. They hide from us (or do not know or have forgotten) that the simple life is the shortest path to happiness. They favor success over happiness, ambition over simplicity, and balance takes a back seat to wealth, power and prestige, which are the underlying cause of the imbalance, both in the community and in the individual.

Why is this ancient inner knowledge, this wisdom not taught to young people in families, schools, social institutions? The exploitative system (and most social systems are exploitative) which by definition rejects this knowledge, makes very well sure that it is estranged, debased and hidden from the exploited masses.

To be able to continue to exploit the masses in peace, it makes sure to numb them with moldy spiritual food such trivial pop culture, 'Gladiator Games' (which professional sport has turned into), stage shows and the advertising industry, in other words, through global mass media marketing which promotes and sells a virtual life that is far from any reality and common sense.

But a freeing consciousness is available to everyone because it is in all of us; moreover, we swim in it like fish in water. Still, we are entertained by the waste that waves have brought out to the coast beyond the ocean of spiritual Consciousness in us. We are trained like seagulls, we rummage through mental garbage and we satisfy our hunger with carcasses instead of discovering the wealth of spiritual life within ourselves.

Unfortunately, vulgar-materialist sciences and a Pharisaic *religious industry* go hand in hand with the exploitative strategies of political and economic systems, they go shoulder to shoulder with its dazzling show-business, for they all strive to make man addicted to the system, or to their *own system* to be more specific, and not to guide him into discovering his own spiritual treasures. This confirms that the liberated man is of no interest to anyone, but to himself, because a man of freedom cannot be manipulated, exploited, lead to be evil and wicked by anyone for their own interests.

An anecdote about the brilliant inventor Nikola Tesla describes this picturesquely. When he offered the banker J. P. Morgan to take part in his revolutionary wireless transmission of energy project, the banker refused to give him any financial support, saying that he could not see how he could get a return on his investment in this particular project.

Such an outlook on life, man and the world is shared by most contemporary exploiters and manipulators who are interested only in filling their ever-hungry belly. Were they to invest their wealth and power in expanding knowledge on how we can draw life, spirit and energy from our treasury, who and what would they be making money off of?

Banks and perfidious extortionists, shopping centers and cheap merchants, churches and religions would go bust; so much of that useless entertainment and beauty industry would go bust for he who has found his Self, all the world's lucidity & beauty belongs to him by nature. He does not need loans, shopping therapy, superstitious litanies and show-business circus performers to entertain it, because he finds all that is good, beautiful and wise and which the purified heart seeks in his own Being.

Were man to turn to the unexplored treasures of his own spirit and away from the deceptive world of illusion in which professional illusionists harness him to their plows like a mute ox to till the land of their illusions, most systems that serve only themselves and their self-preservation would fail at the expense of the deluded and enslaved man.

All that would remain would be that which is most valuable, that with which no one can or is allowed to do trade: the freedom that each individual has to explore, create, get to know and travel his Path.

IX.5 The Son of a Bitch's herostratic victory

The ego is the procurer and the prostitute which it procures, the trader and the expensive goods it offers, the illusionist and the "fog" that it sells... This is what the ego truly is: an unnatural outgrowth in our being, a bump that tries to sell itself for a man, a tumor that presents itself as the surgeon, a parasite that pretends to be a bread-winner, an illusion that blinds the being and in doing so identifies itself as that very being.

The ego is a *Son of a Bitch* who thinks that the world and family, partners, friends and other people exist only for it; that a partner is there to meet its needs or to at least to usuriously do trade with; that offspring are there to be his Majesty's natural extension and are better to not exist at all if they aren't.

The ego is the procurer and the prostitute which it procures, the trader and the expensive goods it offers, the illusionist and the "fog" that it sells, the actor and the show that elicits admiration and longing sighs, the canticles and the rent from the wallets of the naive. The ego is Mephistopheles who seduces Faust's soul, offering it this vain world's glory, taking in return all the best it has: authenticity, sincerity, purity, nobility...

For Mephistopheles there is no greater joy and pleasure than when he breaks a soul, makes it fall to its knees and drags it through the mud. This is what the ego truly is: an unnatural outgrowth in our being, a bump that tries to sell itself for a man, a tumor that presents itself as the surgeon, a parasite that pretends to be a bread-winner, an illusion that blinds the being and in doing so identifies itself as that very being.

And woe to those who do not believe it, who resist it, who engage in trade, bargaining or competition with it, for they have condemned themselves to a lifelong struggle as the ego is a chameleon who will not give up the fight for authority, power and control until the Master of this House (our true Self) strips it of authority, takes away its power, submits it to his control and pulverizes it, as an intruder, back into the mind's dust out of which it hatched out like a moth.

The ego is a bottomless abyss, a cancer of the human soul which spreads faster and more dangerously than a polluted sea. Who does not realize this on time, who groggily dreams on and does not try to fight it off while he still has the strength to do so, this dreamer will eventually be pulled to the bottom of his vanity, to the bottom of the insatiable abyss by the ego who will be exultant in its herostratic victory.

IX.6 Buried under a pile of *emotional corpses*

The first time that man pulled away before the Truth, he overshadowed himself, overshadowed his heart with repressed pain, bitterness, anger... And then, when his own Being could no longer be discerned under the pile of emotional corpses, man may have realized that the path of withdrawal never ends...

Man cannot be dishonest with himself and not suffer because of it. As the conscience is his True Self's moral dimension, man cannot cheat his own conscience without cheating himself.

Acting contrary to his conscience, man acts under the dictates of the "distorted self-image" and so begins to serve the false master of his life, all while forgetting and neglecting his True Being. However, the conscience, which is a sort of self-pronouncement of our True Being, will not give any peace to those who have turned their backs on it, while they are awake or asleep, in this or in the other world, until they are once again turned face-to-face with it.

In the Gnostic Gospel of Thomas, Jesus in several places depicted the state of a man as painfully being divided between his true and false self. Jesus said: "Two will recline on a bed; one will die, one will live..." and then "if one is whole, one will be filled with light, but if one is divided, one will be filled with darkness." (Thomas, 61).

For everything that man has hidden from himself, his infidelity and fraud, deceit and hypocrisy, everything is pushed deep, deep into the reservoir of his subconscious, where he tries to dissociate from the light of his True Being with that *landfill*. Much like someone who *steals* the shore from the ocean with dikes and dams, refusing to accept that sooner or later the ocean would once again flood, man in vain pushes his lies into *self-forgetfulness*, not understanding that his conscience, like a boomerang, will throw them right back in his face.

And the more man deceives himself, the more he pushes himself into the darkness of the unconscious, into the blindness of the separation from the light of his consciousness. Our *conscious* is as extended as we are honest with ourselves, as much as in those moments we accept us *as ourselves*, not renouncing the further development of ourselves in the direction of authenticity and integrity, until the complete awakening and actualization of our True Identity.

The first time we betrayed our Self was when we refused to fight for what our conscience commanded us to, when we pulled back from the attack that tried to separate us from our spiritual essence, grind us like grapes picked off a vine, and reshape us according to the tyrannical ego's will.

The first time that man pulled away before the truth, he overshadowed himself, overshadowed his heart with repressed pain, bitterness, anger... And then, when his own Being could no longer be discerned under the pile of *emotional corpses*, man may have realized that the path of withdrawal never ends... However, then it is usually too late, because the ego, that chimera with a thousand masks but without a face, has long since sat at the heart's throne.

From then on, man's entire life is the mask of adjustment to the will for survival, a travesty subordinated by the survival strategy by consenting to be modeling clay in the hands of others. But in all of these various models, man cannot find the True Being *that he would love and be loved by*.

Unfortunately, man generally does not understand that through the misappropriation of his consciousness and of his heart, he is being led step by step to his spiritual suicide. And until he removes the self-centered ego's deceptive veil from his heart, his soul's history will be nothing but the evolution of a spiritual suicide, attained through different ways and at different prices.

In contrast, Socrates's serene acceptance of the pitcher with poison in it, Jesus's acceptance of the cross, Giordano's acceptance of the pyre, were all physical suicides. Oh but what spiritual liberation in the uncompromising testimony of the Truth that their conscience dictates until their last breath, by when the time of deception and lies ceases forever.

IX.7 The world might not be an illusion, but it is mostly a self-delusion

This is just one of the brief summaries through which we can try to understand why for some spiritual teachings such as Vedanta this world is just a simulacrum or an illusion (maya); certainly not because it is illusory in its material existence, but because we do not see or live its reality; instead, we pass through it, sleeping, in our world of self-delusion.

As soon as man is born, his environment begins to deceive. They teach him how to adapt himself in order to make it easier for them to raise him, and not to allow him to naturally develop and grow. They teach him to be adaptable, not stable; to be useful, not authentic; to be incorporated into the community, not honest. They expect him to be successful, and to keep honesty to himself.

When he submissively accepts that he is being deceived, and usually he has no choice because the manipulation begins in early childhood, that is when the process of self-delusion begins. Man forgets, if he had even awakened in the first place, his true *Self* and begins to create his *persona*, which is tailored to the environment's expectations and to the success he is expected to achieve.

The man who has assented to self-delusion continues to deceive others around himself: his friends, partners and spouses, ancestors and descendants. Everything that he comes in contact with serves the purpose of compensating for his grand unfulfillment and emptiness. Career, hobbies, status symbols and social prestige... everything is there to hide his personal unrealisedness, both from others and from himself. The same goes with his descendants. They are there to be man's *natural* extension, to fulfill all of his shortcomings and failures.

This is a monumental project and burden which is too heavy for the "cadet" who might not have any other ambitions besides becoming the bass player in the local garage *band* or the left-wing in the local football club. But who's asking? His fate is pre-determined and sealed without much consultation, accompanied by the standard explanation that all this is for his safety and good. And that "good" which is worth more than any security or prestige, *personal freedom*, is not included in his life path's map. In culinary terms, this is a *dessert* that is not included on the *menu* and that no one will offer on a platter. To get it, each individual in this system of values will have to fight to the very last breath.

Little by little, the (self)deceived individual's entire micro-world is interconnected by relationships based on interests, manipulation and hypocrisy. If here and there a little honesty is shown, it is just so the targeted victim "opens up" a little and is prepared for an indefensible shot. The life of the self-deceived person who continues to deceive others is insatiably empty. He only cultivates safe and calculated relationships. He only approaches those from whom he can benefit and puts down and pushes away from himself those that could love him. He is too unsettled by those whose feelings force him to open up and to perhaps love. This would be the collapse of the monumental fortress in which he has invested his whole life.

Years go by and the (self)deceived individual slowly realizes that he is as lonely as a *Pharaoh* and that he has built a *mausoleum* in his own home. He has been dead for a long time but, occupied with the recycling of his splendid *persona*, hasn't even had the chance to notice it. Furthermore, he has already been embalmed alive; he only needs to be buried. But even this little deed will not be carried out by anyone, without a bill.

And so, he has no choice but to wait, wait and maybe, if he has not been struck by senility, wonder: Where is the root of this monumental (self)deception we call life? Where did the infinite wrong turns and dawdling begin? But usually it is already too late for profound answers for the one who has spent his life lying to himself and others around him, convinced that he is doing it for the best. All that remains is the hope for an afterlife or for misconceptions to be enlightened in a new incarnation, in which the path that he has passed more than once waits for him again.

This is just one of the brief summaries through which we can try to understand why for some spiritual teachings such as *Vedanta* this world is just a simulacrum or an illusion (*maya*); certainly not because it is illusory in its material existence, but because we do not see or live its *reality*; instead, we pass through it, sleeping, in our world of self-delusion.

X. HE WHO LOSES HIMSELF ALONG THE WAY FINDS THE TRUE PATH

It was as though I were frozen solid in the midst of an ice sheet extending tens of thousands of miles. A purity filled my breast and I could neither go forward nor retreat. To all intents and purposes I was out of my mind and only the koan remained... This state lasted for several days. Then I chanced to hear the sound of the temple bell and I was suddenly transformed.

Description of Japanese Zen Master

Hakuin's awakening experience

Satori brings about an inner transformation of a revolutionary character. The pupil does not notice it at first; only his teacher notices it, and he does not discuss it, but lets it ripen and come to perfection.

Eugen Herrigel: The Method of Zen

X.1 When the awakened man loses himself, he finds the Universe – when a closed barrel loses its bottom, it finds the Source

The true center is not physiological but psychological. It is a state of awareness and un-attachment, of permeability and spontaneous activity which is not motivated by a coveted re-

ward nor inhibited by undesirable consequences, because in its authenticity it is freed of all calculation.

While a child is growing out of its immersion in the *unconscious*, it seeks and finds its support outside of itself: in its parents, educators, friends and environment. When it matures and is able to find a foothold in itself, it first develops its own pseudo-center and seeks a foothold in its own *ego's* values.

But it is very quickly proven that the more inflated the ego, the weaker the inner confidence. This is one of the main causes of the arrogance of young, immature people, which will cause them to be faced with a number of obstacles in life and confirm that this pseudo-center is not and cannot be their genuine foothold, but is primarily the defense system (the *ego-complex*) of their own fears and anxieties before their personal inability to adequately respond to the key challenges of life.

When that system becomes a prison, the individual will have to find the path to freedom. However, the path to freedom often resembles a leap into the uncertain. Courage is needed for that leap, and while pseudo-center ties most of the energy into its own self-defense and survival the individual has neither the strength nor the determination for that uncertain leap. Therefore, the *true nucleus* needs to be found, awoken and activated so that its activities can draw energy from the pseudo-center and return it to its Source.

The true center is not physiological but psychological. It is a state of awareness and unattachment, of permeability and spontaneous activity which is not motivated by a coveted reward nor inhibited by undesirable consequences, because in its authenticity it is freed of all calculation.

In order for this state to be achieved and strengthened, gradual awakening methods, such as breathing, posture and body movement awareness, awareness of a nerve plexus or of a subtle energy center or simply tracking the flow of thought process are used in order for the *mental noise*, which the ego continuously produces in order to constantly remind itself and everything around it that it exists, to be abated and stopped, and for the focus of spiritual activities to be shifted to unmotivated *consciousness per se.*

But no matter which method you use, if you practice meditation persistently and with discipline the pseudo-center will little by little exhaust its defense forces and strategies, the *true nucleus* will be empowered and the egocentric mind will leave its dictatorial position to the balancing *metaposition* (the position beyond the ego's and Shadow's polarities) of awareness.

This is the only way that our True Nature can be increasingly expressed in our every action as well as in all the more noble character of our personalities.

In the end, the state of *Awakening* ebbs and flows like a tide of consciousness when all dams are demolished, when there is no longer a need for any kind of center. The awakened man loses himself but finds the Universe. Metaphorically put: *the closed barrel loses its bottom, but it finds the Source.*

The awakened consciousness flows naturally like a river: it supports everything and undermines nothing, it does not isolate itself nor does it claim anything, it does not own anything but everything inherently belongs to it. And since it gives in to everything without calculation, it fears nothing and hence needs no separate foothold.

But before achieving a permanent state of Awakening, one should develop a strong *center of presence and autonomy*. Furthermore, it represents a prerequisite for a stable research voyage on which, we do not remember when, we set off while we did not yet see this uncertain spiritual odyssey's dock.

X.2 Meditation – the path to the restoration of the unity of Consciousness and its states

Meditation is not a rational/analytical or abstract/intellectual method. Every authentic meditation leads the meditator to the deep spiritual experience of the ego-mind's absence, where it is possible to directly see with the entire being or, in other words, to an experience that transcends the mind's obstructive analytical and conceptual processes.

That which we overlook in everyday observation is that the ego is but a means though it strives to be a leader, forgetting that leadership naturally belongs to our True Being.

But in meditation we can experience a state in which *the ego and the Self, the mind and Consciousness* do not oppose each other but complement each other as objects and space. The *wholeness of existence* needs both because it is Unity: the unity of Consciousness and its states.

In this context, we find that meditation, which leads consciousness's development into one metaposition in which all the conflicting aspects of the mind are balanced and harmonized, is superior to classic Western psychology, psychoanalysis, and various forms of psychotherapy that were formed in the West over the course of the last hundred years. Anyone who has had the opportunity to practically experience, critically examine and impartially compare the possibilities of meditation and psychoanalysis has probably realized that psychoanalysis is not necessary to be able to be freed of the *veil of ignorance* that the ego's defense system covered his fundamental consciousness with. Furthermore, the analysis of mental processes often additionally entangles the *analysand* in the egocentrically oriented mind's network.

Psychoanalysis can *balance* the individuality which is somewhat socially adapted, but not the truly integrated person. The integration process involves the whole person at all levels, from the individual to the universal, and not just the *individuality's organization*. The ancient name for this process is the *Path of Self-Knowledge*. Thus, it is only when we personally experience that we cannot escape the mind's network through methods involving the mind that we are able to practice meditation with our whole being.

Meditation is not a rational/analytical or abstract/intellectual method. Every authentic meditation leads the meditator to the deep spiritual experience of the *ego-mind's absence,* where it is possible to directly see with the entire being or, in other words, to an experience that transcends the mind's obstructive analytical and conceptual processes.

Therefore, in deep meditation the *veil of ignorance* may fall suddenly and without any preparation when our Consciousness accepts all the conditions which it enlightens as manifestations of itself. No meticulous scientific system, philosophical doctrine based on intellectual understanding or religious dogma based on sheer faith is of much help on *the path of meditation.*

This is incomprehensible to the abstract Western mind. Thus classic oriental *objectless meditation* (Sanskrit: *Dhyana,* Chinese: *Ch'an,* Japanese: *Zen*) did not achieve the expected success in the West despite a flourishing initial enthusiasm. A flood of literary titles such as *Zen and Logic, Zen and Quantum Physics, Zen and Navigation* only confirms how far Westerners are from the true experience of the simplicity and naturalness of Eastern meditation and must call for the help of scientific and technical disciplines' power in order to adapt it and approach it to their rational-conceptual minds.

X.3 The mind's unpredictable dynamics and Consciousness's spiraling development

The mandala's defensive structure, which is often obsessively painted by patients with mental health problems, clearly demonstrates the ego's impenetrable defense structure; referring to the simple and often overlooked fact that ego is its own defensive structure. The ego's collapse is the ultimate collapse of that defensive structure out of which a new, awakened man can resurge; but also, behind this structure, only a pile of rubble can remain.

When the universal Self's *dynamic principle* or creative force is separated from its *static center* or creative Consciousness in the process of creation manifestation, that is when each individual form of the Self must create a transitional individual center or a *temporary center* because it has lost conscious contact with the *universal center* during creation's manifestation and evolution processes.

That moment of losing contact is the moment of dynamic principles' separation from its static center; but only as a manner of speaking, taking into consideration that the universal Self's consciousness is omnipresent and therefore cannot have a factual center. Here the center will be called the imaginary point of unity of *Consciousness and power*, of the *static and dynamic principles*, although this unity in reality never was nor can be lost. Due to cosmic manifestations, i. e. cosmic illusions, we simply forgot about it. In this context, a return to the original unity is the awakening from illusion and the identification with unimpaired Oneness.

But let us return to the moment where *contact was lost*, which is experienced by the individual consciousness that is confined by the limits of individual forms in which it was manifested. From that moment onwards, the dynamic power of each individual being must be channeled to a *temporary center*, which is just a slightly better or slightly worse substitute for the loss of (or forgetting about) the *universal center*. For the mystic who seeks to restore the original unity *through love*, that center is God. For the gnostic who seeks that same unity *through cognition*, that center is the absolute Self.

Regardless of how long this return can take and despite the temporary center's or ego's wandering, the deeper intuition (*prajna*) within each being constantly takes him back to the transpersonal Source for each being subconsciously suspects that there lies the fullness of the actualization od his unawakened potential. This potential sleeps in Consciousness's unawakened pole (the so-called *unconscious pole*) which the individual mind that is misled by the limited notion of a temporary *ego* isn't aware of.

However, these potentials spontaneously aspire to actualize themselves in the psyche's *conscious field*. This aspiration drives the individual mind, and in doing so it expands the ego's frames and borders (more precisely, personal consciousness's borders limited by the ego's notion of itself and of the world). Since the intellect (buddhi) is the dynamics of the mind's helmsman and the *unconscious field* is a source of mental energy reserves or the driving force of those dynamics, the ego, as the metaphorical *captain* of this navigation, is forced to constantly adjust to the *mind's dynamics* if it wants to survive.

In this adaptation the ego transforms himself until it has exhausted all adaptation possibilities (read: *dodging* possibilities). That is when a whole, integrated Consciousness, in the spreading of its potential, simply makes it overflow or transcends it. Namely, when the mind's dynamics reaches its peak in the constant actualization of its possibilities, *the helmsman and the captain* (*intellect and the ego*) become redundant. The path is now wide open and transparent and the mind's dynamic power naturally and intuitively returns to its center or the Source.

Still, the function of ego is necessary while the *unconscious* field outweighs the *conscious field* in the psyche; for the ego that imposes itself as the organizational center of the *conscious field* (and identifies with this function) experiences pressure from the *power of the unconscious* as a threat to its own survival. It therefore builds a complex defense system around the *conscious field* to control the influx and outflow of the *unconscious field's* power/content.

The *mandala's* defensive structure, which is often obsessively painted by patients with mental health problems, clearly demonstrates the ego's impenetrable defense structure; referring to the simple and often overlooked fact that ego is *its own defensive structure*. The ego's collapse is the ultimate collapse of that defensive structure out of which a new, *awakened man* can resurge; but also, behind this structure, only a *pile of rubble* can remain.

Once the *conscious field* outweighs the *unconscious* in the mind's personal dynamic, the ego is no longer necessary because the *intuitive mind* that is freed by the powerful expansion of consciousness knows the right path to its *origin*. However, if the ego-structure "cracks" under the pressure of unconscious forces before the *conscious field* is wide enough to integrate the flow of unconscious content, individuality will drown in the sea of *non-integrated unconscious* losing its individual center while not having yet found its universal core.

In such circumstances we cannot talk about the awakening of higher progressive states of consciousness, but of the split in the singular personality and its occupation by consciousness's regressive states. This shows that in the mind's unpredictable dynamics the development of consciousness does not take linear but a spiral path, through a succession of ups and downs, alternating between paths and side roads, back to the original source.

X.4 The path to the return to the Source: from the power given by control to the fulfillment that is achieved through devotion

This radical change arises when man realizes that the ego's structure is merely a model that has the function of a Potemkin facade whose only purpose is hiding its emptiness from the world and from itself. Then it is possible to have the devotion that will overcome the need for control and that, in giving itself into its Source, will achieve the highest possible pleasure, finding personal fulfillment in self-forgetfulness.

By observing without adhering and identifying with consciousness's modes which include thoughts, feelings, desires, drives, etc., the awakened observer can stir the deeply repressed, unconscious motivation that drives these modes.

That underlying motivation can be identified in the young child. The child simultaneously wants power and pleasure, but before colliding with socially-conditioned reality it will have to learn that it cannot have both at once; for if its satisfaction depends on outside factors it will soon realize that in exchange for pleasure it must give up the innate desire for power and vice versa; if it wants to affirm its own will for power it will have to give up pleasure.

With time, the child grows up and with the development of individuality, with aspirations for autonomy and with the emancipation of the ego, the will for power competes with the desire for pleasure. In order to free himself from this trap, the young person develops a specific *control strategy*. This strategy entails that he has to control the external circumstances, as well as internal states, in order to maintain his power and also feel pleasure.

On the basis of such a strategy, the ego builds its own double-wall defense structure: towards the external world of the social and towards the inner world of the mental, therefore making himself the *supreme controller*, but also a *prisoner* of this control. And so, due to its own emancipation, the ego at first tries to control the body and the mind, with the environment and internal states. But eventually, having become a slave to its own control, it will seek freedom by getting rid of the burden which he is to himself. In the end the *controller*, after he is forced to submit control, finally realizes that this whole time *he* was not the director and the spectator of the game; his Source or *Self* was.

The direct way for man to free himself of the control and burden of his ego is:

a. an exploration of the structure and of the way the mind and the ego function,

b. followed by a complete shift in mentally-focused energy's attention from the ego's false construction to the Source from which a continuous stream of consciousness flows along with all its manifestations, which includes the world, the individual, the mind, objects, the ego...

This radical change arises when man realizes that the *ego's structure* is merely a model that has the function of a Potemkin facade whose only purpose is hiding its emptiness from the world and from itself. Then it is possible to have the devotion that will overcome the need for control and that, in *giving itself into* its Source, will achieve the highest possible pleasure, finding personal fulfillment in *self-forgetfulness.*

Without this shift in the center of his own being, like a child man would play with masks until the end of time, he would never get to know his Original Face.

X.5 The true intelligence is actually the awakening of consciousness

It is possible to understand such limiting discord between the grandiose theoretical capacities of intellect and a lack of practical wisdom if in a direct contemplative manner we realize that intellect is not intelligence, and that true intelligence is actually the awakening of consciousness

Man can be an extraordinary intellectual yet a man may still remain blind to reality, may continue living in the dream or in the illusion that is created by *a network of impressions*, by their classification and labels and identification with the labels; in other words, the virtual network that is being continually reproduced by the mind's and intellect's unconscious activities.

Often these intellectual "know-it-alls" do not show the least bit of prudence, let alone wisdom in crucial life situations; rather they act according to one of the many pre-planned schemes that are continuously created by their mighty intellect. Postmodern thought and art, which is mostly created by such abstract intellectuals, clearly testifies to the sad realization *that the more abstract the human mind is, the more life seems absurd to them*. It is no wonder that the post-modern culture of abstract intellectualism has become borderline absurd, for intellect that is not founded in reality actually functions like label factory for non-existent products.

It is possible to understand such limiting discord between the grandiose theoretical capacities of intellect and a lack of practical wisdom if in a direct contemplative manner we realize that intellect is not intelligence, and that true intelligence is actually the *awakening of consciousness*; if we accept that it is only through the awakening of consciousness that man attains deeper wisdom, i. e. the ability to experience circumstances in their internal relationship and not only in their superficial manifestation.

On the other hand, a man of average intellectual capacity but with well-developed soberness and attention can sooner attain practical life wisdom, for instead of getting entangled in the net of his own thoughts to which every ambitious thinker eventually becomes prey, he observes wakefully and impartially and so the nature of things effortlessly reveals itself to him.

The key to this is understanding without unnecessary thinking, whereby the power of impartial observation goes beyond the efforts of violent reasoning. Thus, the Whole reflects itself to the conscious observer because he does not try to dissect it as the mind of the smug intellectual aggressively does. The latter, when he fragments a pure vision of the whole with his conceptual schemes, continues dawdling like a fool, not knowing what to do with the dead intellectual debris.

The path to the awakening of consciousness is easy and direct but it cannot be taught or learned for the *path to consciousness* develops with internal maturity; it primarily requires our presence, and development unfolds on its own. Presence brings us the simplicity that includes modesty.

Since true modesty exists with no big expectations, it accepts the phenomena and circumstances as they come before it. This is how inartificial naturalness and pure spontaneity are born. Since naturalness in itself is *complete*, it lacks nothing. This is how unattachment is born. In detachment there is no partition into the *ego and others, higher and lower, inner and outer, past and future...* And so out of unattachment springs the awakening of consciousness.

X.6 Taking responsibility is the only cure for the unbearable emptiness of the *imitation of life*

A new life is an awakening that no longer cares for the nightmares and the sweet dreams that were dreamt; it is the blossoming of our True Being which, selfishly in love with a false self-image, we too long kept fasting and without light offered by the attention of consciousness which is liberated from the veil of dreaming and reasoning.

It is only from that point that one can begin to develop, branch out and blossom into a *new life*; and that life is a completely different story that has nothing in common with the previous one. That life is a 180 degree turn and an upstream navigation going against the current.

While someone else is taking responsibility for our actions, life seems like a game to us. When we begin to take responsibility ourselves and bear the consequences of our own decisions and for the way we live, we start to shape out character. We shape it with our own will; not with the environment's will or through a series of coincidences that life brings before us like driftwood.

Avoiding responsibility most certainly prolongs the emotional immaturity of people and forms an infantile personality that today's *culture of superficiality* is rife with. And the mega-popularity of soap operas and soap-bubble characters only confirms the immaturity of our civilization, and the infantilism that is not of global but of cosmic proportions.

Furthermore, that culture of superficiality encourages and celebrates infantile personalities, making them the idols of our age, because they are built with a lack of personality and integrity and are appropriate material for lucrative show-business; first and foremost because they have no personality, no character, no authentic identity and therefore have the ideal personality type for being clowns, entertainers and drama queens as well as mass media puppets in which everyone can *see* what they need, in which anyone can project the attributes they desire in their own unrealized identities.

In reality their lives are nothing more than "*a tale told by an idiot, full of sound and fury, signifying nothing*" (as Shakespeare said in *Macbeth*) or an *empty bubble*, which must constantly be filled with alcohol, drugs and scandals... The emptiness of all these *imitations of life* is so unbearable that the only possible cure is to take responsibility for one's attitudes and actions and to stand behind them with one's whole being, regardless of the price to pay.

It is only from that point that one can begin to develop, branch out and blossom into a *new life*; and that life is a completely different story that has nothing in common with the previous one. That life is a 180 degree turn and an upstream navigation going against the current.

A new life is an awakening that no longer cares for the nightmares and the sweet dreams that were dreamt; it is the blossoming of our True Being which, selfishly in love with a false self-image, we too long kept fasting and without light offered by the attention of consciousness which is liberated from the veil of dreaming and reasoning.

X.7 He who loses himself *along the way* finds the true *Path*

In the third stage, the seeker becomes aware of how much this "image of me" deadens him (denying him the vitality and spontaneity of life), frustrates him (because he cannot meet the high standards that the image sets), and limits him (for due to the "image" he cannot see the real I's dormant potential that's waiting to be awakened and actualized).

Whoever frees himself of *ego-consciousness* (awareness of the self in terms of the image we have of ourselves) finds *true consciousness which in itself* is free of preconceptions about the world and the *ego*. Whoever forgets about their *concept of self* also finds their deepest *Individuality*.

The limited, conditioned *ego* cannot get to know the unlimited, unconditional *Self*. The mind limited by the individual cannot get to know the authentic, absolute Consciousness. Where there is a pairing of subject and object of knowledge, how can the *True Nature* of the "knower" flourish?

From the ego to the non-ego, from the mind to the no-mind, from the world of countless different phenomena to the world of undifferentiated *emptiness*, the *pendulum* of *adhesion and rejection* swings without stopping, and karma's clock keeps on ticking. Neither the ego the non-ego, neither the mind nor the no-mind, neither manifestation nor emptiness is the *core* of all the Path's *states* without adhesion and rejection, without intent, goals and expectations. The Path is just the *here and now*, the point from which the pendulum swings and returns to...

Whoever builds a consistent *picture of himself* also enslaves himself because he has to invest a great amount of energy in order to keep that image stable in the eyes others as well as in his own (if he does not believe in it himself, who else will?), and that is why man's ego is so exhaustingly difficult. He who does not care about his *image* does not waste time, attention and energy on the meaningless game of masks and mirrors. That is why he can live as spontaneous and unrestrained as the wind, as inexhaustible as the source.

The ego craves an ideal concept of life and of itself, but that notion constantly eludes it because it is unrealistic, as is the ego after all. It persistently hunts that *notion*, but grasps onto air each time, much like the hand that catches cannot catch itself, like a sword that cuts cannot cut itself, like the eye that sees cannot see itself.

Life responds to its aggressive ambition in such a way that it brings it everything that it despised and rejected in its Shadow. That is why only he who lives without an image of himself can get what he needs on his Path. But let the pendulum be a little troubled, let consciousness's balance be perturbed, let ambitions and desires only poke their heads out of the basement and let's finally witness that behind them they automatically draw the projections (*vikshepa*) from the unconscious mind to the world of objects, reopening the vicious cycle of illusion.

Therefore, he who steps onto this Path must cease building and sustaining self-notions, such as: *"I should be different and not the way I am!" "I should live a fuller life and not the one I live!" "I deserve better than what I have!"* etc., etc.... For all that is a priori the *Path's choreographies* and maps that reliably lead to the goal, will be revealed to the observant seeker as burdensome and flawed.

Instead of complicated strategies, the following is sufficient:

- to be present
- to travel without a plan
- to contemplate without expectations.

Such a Path is simple, direct and free of the binding baggage and excessive burden that many travelers burden themselves with, until they ultimately perish under the weight of grandiose projects.

But above all, at a certain point on the Path, the traveler must identify how much his own egocentrism inhibits him and must be able to dismiss it. This means freeing himself of *self-consciousness* and letting the authentic consciousness within him flourish along the journey.

If we succeed in freeing ourselves of the states and characteristics that our *self-adoring* ego adheres to daily, we will forget about ourselves spontaneously and without much counterproductive effort. For he who forgets himself loses himself step by step; and he who loses himself *along the way* finds the true Path.

The seeker goes through a number of phases on the path to consciousness:

a. In the first, he lives and acts instinctively and affectively, without clear self-insight and idea about how he should act. This is the *unconscious* life.

b. In the second phase, the seeker tries to bring instincts and affects under control, in line with the notion he developed of his own characteristics and values, in other words, in accordance with the "image" (imago) he has built of himself. This is the *ego-conscious* life.

c. In the third stage, the seeker becomes aware of how much this "image of me" deadens him (denying him the vitality and spontaneity of life), frustrates him (because he cannot meet the high standards that the image sets), and limits him (for due to the "image" he cannot see the real I's dormant potential that's waiting to be awakened and actualized).

It is only when he realizes this and is able to, through the process of meditation and contemplation, deprive of the energy of attention that "dead image" which maintains itself on life and draws on his life's vitality; it is only when he refocuses his attention and with it its consciousness and energy in search of his True Self that a *conscious life* becomes possible.

Only then does the true Path start, which can be summarized in three verses:

> *Be what you are,*
> *accept what comes,*
> *let it go along – its Path.*

AFTERWORD

All teachings and writings are only markers,
we must cross the Path ourselves

These insights resulted from the expression of a practical contemplative "self-mirroring" on the Path to Self-knowledge and therefore their primary goal is to offer others topics to consider, incentives for personal self-reflection, to be a reminder of the individual sections of the Path that the traveler passes lightly; and that there are no shortcuts to the True Being's blossoming or a surrogate (neither theoretical nor technical) that could replace personal experience in that blossoming process.

This is not a textbook written by academic philosophers whose intention is to instruct students and impress colleagues. This is a practical *guide on the Path* that unscrupulously targets demasking lightly adopted psychological and social conditions.

The book is comprised of concise essays, insights and self-reflections which have arisen over the course of many years of theoretical and practical research on Eastern and Western paths to self-knowledge, with a special emphasis on Hindu (Vedanta, Yoga and Kashmir Shaivism) and Buddhist (Zen, Tibetan *Mahamudra* and *Vijnanavada* schools of Mahayana Buddhism) doctrines and methods of Eastern tradition (in this context, India is the prime meridian that divides the Eastern and Western spiritual hemisphere).

As for Western tradition, in the philosophical sense we undoubtedly owe most to ancient Greek schools of wisdom (from Heraclitus and Parmenides to the Stoics and Plotinus's Neo-Platonism), to the revolutionary *philosopher of will* Arthur Schopenhauer and the lucid *philosopher of the Path* Alan Watts; to Christian and Sufi Gnosticism on the spiritual plan; to spiritually oriented schools of Western psychology such as Carl Gustav Jung's depth psychology and George Ivanovich Gurdjieff's esoteric psychology.

The specifics of Eastern teachings were clarified in the spirit of depth psychology and in the language of Western Philosophy where necessary, because without a proper "translation" into the cultural context in which the mind of the average Westerner is formed there cannot be a proper understanding or correct application of these teachings. On the other hand, without practicing some of the Eastern methods of self-development, there is no subtler understanding of the layered shades of the doctrine that supports those methods. Therefore, in the text there is a balance between *knowledge and experience*; thus remaining true to the position that doctrine and method must support one another, just like both wings harmoniously support a bird's flight.

To more easily connect the individual sections of the Path, the reflections were grouped into ten thematic sections (such as "Freedom beyond the mind and time", "The passage through the deceptive veil of illusion", "An empty cocoon from the start", etc.) which can be read as individual insights. The first five *units/insights* deal with the enlightenment of our internal processes and states, and the last five with revealing the subtle manipulations that govern our external relations;

for without a balance between the internal and the external, there is no true understanding of the Path.

These sudden *illuminations* spontaneously arose from meditation, from the consideration of individual sections on the Path, from attempts to untangle internal knots and conflicts or were triggered by the desire to share certain observations with other seekers on the timeless path of self-knowledge. They do not stem from pretention in order to create one more imperfect *map to the Path* or a rounded philosophical doctrine, and they are not burdened with the ballast *textbook* footnotes.

One of the most brilliant interpreters of paths of self-knowledge as well as a brilliant and concise stylist, British philosopher Alan Watts, long ago ironized *academic* writing about matters which in their nucleus resist the abstraction academic categories, calling it *"square Zen"*. Therefore, as far as style is concerned, an advantage was given to authorial character and temperament (well-aware of imperfection and flaws) over polished but impersonal and unrelated-to-life academic metaphysics. The guide resulted from the expression of a practical contemplative "self-mirroring" on the Path to self-knowledge and therefore its primary goal is to offer others topics to consider, incentives for personal self-reflection, to be a reminder of the individual sections of the Path that the traveler passes lightly; and that there are no shortcuts to the True Being's blossoming or a surrogate (neither theoretical nor technical) that could replace personal experience in that blossoming process.

In addition, attention was drawn to some of the crucial illusions and delusions which society, civilization and (quasi)culture have been manipulating the individual with from the beginning of mankind and that we blindly accept simply because we spend most of our lives as unconscious slaves to our habits and set conditions.

Most of the specific philosophical, spiritual and psychological terms are briefly explained in the glossary. The Eastern terms used in the text are mainly in Sanskrit, unless otherwise stated. Although most of these teachings have a precisely developed terminology, the language of parables and metaphors was favored over categories. In this context, under the title of each reflection there is an excerpt that illustrates the reflection's main point, as to leave a *poetic trace* that will lead the reader's intuition to his own personal Path.

For the language of parables and metaphors (like Zen koans) does not serve to explain everything to the reader in detail; this would merely be an intellectual explanation that cannot awaken an inner transformation in anybody. The language of parables and koans is a seed planted in the unconscious field of the person it is directed at. This seed does not give immediate results, but if the seeker is diligent in his search, that seed will one day flourish, ripen, and bear the fruit of Awakening in him.

Lessons can inspire and direct us, but only personal insight can permanently change us; that is why all teachings and writings are only markers. We must cross the path ourselves; and this is an experience that cannot be replaced by any intellectual elaboration.

It is wonderful to *look* around oneself while travelling, but it is even more wonderful to occasionally pause, drain oneself of all ambition and expectation and simply – *see*.

GLOSSARY

Actualism – philosophical view according to which reality is not based on a fixed static Being, rather its essence is constant change; a creative and cognitive activity that is continuously undergoing self-realisation, in other words, that progresses from a state of possibility to one of actuality. The originator of this idea is the father of dialectics – Heraclitus. In modern philosophy, some aspects of actualism can be found in the works of the French philosopher Henri Bergson and the British philosopher Alfred North Whitehead.

Analysand – psychoanalytic term for a client who undergoes psychoanalysis.

Avarana – in Hindu philosophy it represents the veil of deception and ignorance with which manifest creation hides the true nature of unconditional consciousness or the Self.

Herostratus – the Greek who set one of the Seven Wonders of the Ancient World, the temple of Artemis at Ephesus, on fire just to get his name recorded in history. A metaphor for the man who does not shy away from dark glory to validate his egotism.

Chthonic – the dark, unconscious and unintegrated aspect of the human psyche that is often depicted through the symbols of snakes and dragons in the myths of ancient civilizations and later alchemical interpretations.

Introjection – the unconscious adoption of the courts' and of external authority's views as one's own.

Ego-Complex – in the psychology of Carl Gustav Jung, this is the complex of the feelings, images and ideas that forms the centre of our field of consciousness. The Ego-complex is also the basis of the sense of personal identity and a continuity of personality.

Self – in Jung's psychology, it is the true nucleus of our psyche, but also the whole of our mental potential.

Camelot – the legendary castle from the myth of King Arthur and his Knights of the Round Table. A symbol of utopian brotherhood dedicated to the knight's life and to spiritual ideals.

Karma – in Hindu and Buddhist philosophy, it is the law of cause and effect that inexorably binds all beings to their own thoughts and feelings, desires and actions. An unbroken karmic chain is the fundamental cause of a number of consecutive (re)incarnations.

Koan – the paradoxical question that the Zen teacher asks the student in order to get an answer from him that is beyond the discriminatory mind and conceptual thinking, an answer that comes from within the entire being or the "no mind" (Chinese: wu-hsin, Japanese: mushin). The teacher can use a variety of koans in order to deepen the student's understanding of the Path, to bring him to enlightenment (Japanese: satori) in the end. The koans that were used by the great Zen teachers for generations are compiled in two main collections: the *Gateless Gate* (Japanese: Mumonkan) and *Blue Cliff Record* (Japanese: Hekiganroku).

Kyudo – the art of shooting arrows from a Japanese bow. In Japan it is classified under one of the traditional *Budo* arts (Way of the Warrior). Primarily a martial art, under the influence of Zen it was transformed into a *path to self-realization*.

Latency – the seclusion phase of potential manifestations in their periods of inertia or non-response.

Mahamudra – means "Great seal" in Sanskrit. Refers to the teachings and meditation practices that were brought to Tibet by the successors of Tilopa, the 10th century Indian teacher of Tantric Buddhism.

Mahat – in the philosophies of Yoga and Vedanta, *mahat* is the cosmic intelligence, the universal Mind or the first aspect of the manifested absolute reality, defined as: Being-Consciousness-Bliss (Sat-Chit-Ananda). In Kashmir Shaivism, it refers to the energy of awareness or *Chitishakti*.

Mandala – the psychological and cosmological diagram of man and the universe which symbolically represents their interdependence. The mandala was originally found in Tantric Buddhism and Hinduism where it was used as a subtle object of meditation. Jung studied mandalas in order to better understand the dynamic structure of the human psyche at the symbolic level.

Maya – the cosmic illusion that hides the true nature of all beings, or Brahman. In Hindu philosophy, this term was mainly used by the Vedanta and Tantric schools, while schools of Yoga use a similar but not synonymous term – prakriti.

Moloch – the ancient god of the Canaanite nation who was presented with human sacrifices, mostly children. Here it is interpreted in psychological terms, as a symbol of the False Self to whom the misguided man sacrifices the best of his authenticity, which is picturesquely represented by the purity and innocence of a child. In modern interpretations, Moloch is the callous mechanism of corrupt political and economic systems that metaphorically and literally feed, reproduce and maintain themselves through a living human sacrifice through a system of ideological manipulation, seduction wars, economic exploitation, etc.

Narcissus – the young man of Greek myth who was killed because of his conceited love for his own beauty. In depth psychology, it is the symbol of an isolating obsession with oneself that leads to stagnation in physical development, and to psychological regression in pathological forms.

Neurotic reductionism – the process of psychological self-preservation in which the individual that is confronted with unsolvable conflicts and crises resorts to reducing the complexity of spiritual life to life's basic functions for a period of time.

Nirvana – in the Buddhist doctrine it means the extinction of desire (*trishna*) for existence and the consequent final liberation (*moksha*) from the cycle of death and rebirth (*samsara*).

Panpsychism – philosophical view according to which the entire universe is pervaded by one, cosmic soul. In Renaissance Neo-Platonism it was represented by Francesco Patrizi and Giordano Bruno.

Prakasha and Vimarsha – Kashmir Shaivism philosophy explains these two functions of consciousness as a simultaneous and complementary. *Prakasha* means the consciousness' ability to illuminate objects it detects, whereas *Vimarsha* is the ability to simultaneously identify them.

Pralaya – in Hindu cosmology it represents the withdrawal of manifest creation into a state of latency once the three cosmic attributes or three gunas (*rajas, tamas, sattva*) are in perfect balance.

Uncertainty principle – in quantum physics it was discovered by the German physicist Werner Heisenberg. This principle describes the movement of particles in the subatomic world, finding that it is not possible to accurately determine both the location and speed of the particles.

Original Face – in Zen Buddhist tradition, the Original Face is a metaphor for our real and innate, enlightened nature, also called the Buddha Nature.

Self-actualization – in broad terms it is the process of making present the potential for personal growth, which previously existed only as a predisposition. In more specific terms, it is the fundamental concept behind humanistic psychologist Abraham Maslow's theory of personalities. For him, self-actualization is the "acceptance and expression of the inner core or *self*," or in other words, the full realization and use of the capacities and resources that are available to someone.

Self-illuminating consciousness – a metaphor for the Self or our True Nature. Vedanta teacher Ramana Maharshi said that the Self is the Heart that illuminates itself. The Pratyabhijna school of Kashmir Shaivism explains that the Supreme Reality (*bhairava*) is self-illuminating (*prakasha-vimarsha*).

Samsara – the manifested world that due to the resulting spiritual illusion and ignorance enslaves all beings in consecutive cycles of birth and death until they liberate themselves from the law of cause and effect.

Scientism – an outlook on man and on the world that prefers a so-called objective-scientific perception of reality, often negating the value of each man's subjective experience (radical scientism).

Ego-consciousness – a self-monitoring and divisive *consciousness of oneself* in terms of set, restrictive *images of the self* as opposed to a spontaneous, unique and limitless consciousness (*self-awareness*) which is our real Self.

Substancialism – the philosophical doctrine that sees the ultimate reality as the foundation of all phenomena and all events in one and indivisible, infinite and eternal substance. The history of philosophy has seen many different variants of substancialism, from Parmenides through Spinoza to Fichte and Hegel.

Tantra – teachings that combine a set of esoteric practices and doctrines that were developed within Buddhism, Shaivism and Brahmanism between the 6th and 13th centuries. Translated from Sanskrit, it literally means *the removal of the darkness of ignorance*. The common characteristic of all tantric teachings is the emphasis on the feminine principle (*shakti*); in other words, the aspect of the force or energy of the *Supreme Reality*.

Transference – psychoanalytic term that roughly means the transfer of the patient's unconscious emotions (most often harnessed towards the parents) to a therapist. The redirection of feelings from a therapist to a patient is called *countertransference*. In broad terms, transference is the transfer of unresolved internal conflicts from the intimate to the social realm. The founder of psychoanalysis, Sigmund Freud, believed that psychoanalysis was not possible without transference because transference was the battleground on which conflicting psychological forces met.

The Upanishads – the philosophical lessons and discussions (traditionally, 108 Upanishads are referred, although there are more) that dialectically review and clarify, usually in the form of a dialogue or lyrics, the thoughts and beliefs passed down for centuries in the Vedas. They were created during the period between the 8th century BCE and the beginning of the new era.

Vedanta – translated from Sanskrit it literally means the *end of knowledge* (*veda* = knowledge, *anta* = end). It is one of the six traditional schools (*darshan*) of Indian philosophy. The teachings of Vedanta are considered the flower of Indian thought and a summary of the tradition of the Vedas and Upanishads. There are three schools of Vedanta: dualism, nondualism and so-called qualified nondualism (the attitudes of the latter make it similar to *Western pantheism*). Here we refer to the Non-dualistic Vedanta teachings whose main representatives are Gaudapada and Shankara and which impart the oneness of the individual soul (*atman*) and the absolute Self/Being (*Brahman*). In modern times these teachings were distinctively and highly practically interpreted by guru Ramana Maharshi (1879-1950).

Vijnanavada – one of the two main schools of Mahayana Buddhism whose teachings were developed by the brothers Asanga and Vasubandhu. The Vijnanavada School, also known as *Yogacara*, denies the realism of material phenomena and the reality creation. Only consciousness is real (*chitta* or *vijnana*) and creations are but its mode of manifestation. In doctrinal terms, these teachings are similar to Non-dualistic Vedanta, and to Yoga in practical terms.

Vikshepa – in Hindu philosophy it is the mind's projections whose intrinsic attributes are attributed to so-called objective phenomena. Simply put, everything we see and experience in the external world is nothing but the projection of karmic seeds stored in the form of impressions and desires in our unconscious. This activity of the mind obscures the true nature of the Self (see – *Avarana*).

A NOTE ABOUT THE AUTHOR

Asanga Angya (b. 1967) philosopher, religiologist and writer, was raised and educated in Europe, where he graduated in Philosophy and Religious Studies. Since 1990 he has been working in print and electronic media and has published numerous essays in the field of philosophy and spirituality, psychology and art. He is the author of a books of spiritual poetry and essays, philosophical novels and scientific screenplays, which were made into films.

For over three decades he has explored traditional Eastern and Western ways of Self-knowledge as well as the practice of Vedanta and Zen meditation in comparison with the modern teachings of depth psychology. Some insights and observations from these studies are summarized in this collection of short essays.

RECOMMENDED LITERATURE

ABE, M.: Zen and Western Thought, University of Hawaii Press, Honolulu, 1985.

ADDIS, S.: Zen sourcebook: Traditional Dokuments from China, Korea, and Japan, Hackett Publishing, Indianapolis, 2008.

AUROBINDO, S.: Letters on Yoga I-II, Lotus Press, Pondicherry, 1995.

AUROBINDO, S.: The Synthesis of Yoga, Lotus Press, Pondicherry, 1990.

AUSTIN, J. H.: Zen and the Brain: Toward an Understanding of Meditation and Consciousness, The MIT Press, 1999.

BASSUI, T.: Mud and Water, Wisdom Publications, Boston, 2002.

BOHM, D.: Wholeness and the Implicate Order, Routledge, 2002.

CAPRA, F.: The Tao of Physics, Shambhala, 2010.

CHATTERJI, J. C.: Kashmir Shaivaism, State University of N. Y., 1986.

EDINGER, E. F.: Anatomy of the Psyche, Open Court Publishing, 1994.

FORD, J. I. & BLACKER, M. M.: The Book of Mu, Wisdom Publications, Boston, 2011.

FRANKL, V. E.: The Doctor and the Soul: From Psychotherapy to Logotherapy, Vintage, 1986.

FUNG YU-LAN: A Short History of Chinese Philosophy, Macmillan, N. Y., 1958.

GOVINDA, L. A.: Foundations of Tibetan Mysticism, Weiser Books, 1969.

GURDJIEFF, G. I.: Life Is Real Only Then, When I Am, Penguin Books, 1999.

HASKEL, P.: Bankei Zen, Grove Press, N. Y., 1984.

HEISENBERG, W.: Physics and Philosophy, Harper, 2007.

HERRIGEL, E.: The Method of Zen, Vintage Books, 1974.

IZUTSU, T.: Toward a Philosophy of Zen Buddhism, Prajna Press, Boulder, 1982.

JIANG, T.: Yogacara Buddhism and Modern Psychology on the Subliminal Mind, University of Hawaii Press, Honolulu, 2006.

JUNG, C. G.: The Archetypes and the Collective Unconscious, Princeton, 1981.

JUNG, C. G.: Symbols of Tranformation, Princeton, 1977.

JUNG, C. G.: The Undiscovered Self, Signet, 2006.

KAWAI, H.: Buddhism and the Art of Psychotherapy, Texas A&M University Press, 2008.

KRISHNAMURTI, J. & BOHM, D.: The Ending of Time, Harper, San Francisco, 1985.

LOORI, J. D.: The Zen of Creativity, Ballantine Books, N. Y., 2005.

MAGID, B.: Ordinary Mind: Exploring the Common Ground of Zen and Psychoanalysis, Wisdom Publications, Boston, 2005.

MASLOW, A.: Motivation and Personality, Harper & Row, N. Y.,1976.

MEYER, M.: The Nag Hammadi Scriptures, Harper One, N. Y., 2009.

MORINAGA, S.: Novice to Master, Wisdom Publications, Boston, 2002.

NEEDHAM, J.: Science and Civilisation in China, Cambridge University Press, 1956.

NIETZSCHE, F.: The Will to Power, Random House, 1973.

OSBORNE, A.: The Teachings of Ramana Maharshi, Weiser Inc., Maine, 1996.

OSBORNE, A.: Ramana Maharshi and the Path of Self-Knowledge, Sophia Perennis, 2006.

OUSPENSKY, P. D.: In Search of the Miraculous, Mariner Books, 2001.

OUSPENSKY, P. D.: The Fourth Way, Vintage, 1971.

PERLS, F. S.: Gestalt Therapy: Excitement and Growth in the Human Personality, The Gestalt Journal Press, 2011.

RADHAKRISHNAN, S.: Indian Philosophy, Allen & Unwin, London, 1951.

REICH, W.: Character Analysis, Farrar, Straus and Giroux, 1980.

SAHN, Seung: The Compass of Zen, Shambhala, Boston, 1997.

SAHN, Seung: Only Don't Know, Shambhala, Boston, 1999.

SAHN, Seung: Wanting Enlightenment Is a Big Mistake, Shambhala, Boston, 2006.

SCHROBE, R.: Don't-Know Mind: The Spirit of Korean Zen, Shambhala, Boston, 2004.

SCHOPENHAUER, A.: The World as Will and Representation, Dover Publications, 2000.

SEKIDA, K.: Zen Training: Methods and Philosophy, Shambhala, Boston, 2005.

SEKIDA, K.: Two Zen Classics: Mumonkan and Hekiganroku, Shambhala, Boston, 2005.

SHIBAYAMA, Z.: A Flower Does Not Talk, Tuttle Company, 1972.

SOENG, M.: Trust in Mind: The Rebellion of Chinese Zen, Wisdom Publications, Boston, 2004.

SOGYAL, R.: The Tibetan Book of Living and Dying, Harper, San Francisco, 2012.

SPEETH, K. R.: The Gurdjieff Work, Tarcher, 1988.

SUNIM, D.: No River to Cross, Wisdom Publications, Boston, 2007.

SUZUKI, D. T.: Manual of Zen Buddhism, Grove Press, N. Y.

SUZUKI, D. T.: The Zen Doctrine of No Mind, Weiser Books, 1991.

SUZUKI, D. T.: Zen and Japanese Culture, Princeton University Press, 2010.

TAKUAN, S.: The Unfettered Mind, Kodansha International, 2006.

TARTHANG, Tulku: Openness Mind, Dharma Publishing, 1990.

VIVEKANANDA, S.: Vedanta Voice of Freedom, Vedanta Society of St Louis, 1990.

WATTS, A. W.: The Spirit of Zen, Grove Press, 1958.

WATTS, A. W.: The Way of Zen, Vintage, 1999.

WU, J. C. H.: The Golden Age of Zen: Zen Masters of the T'ang Dynasty, World Wisdom, 2003.

www.ingramcontent.com/pod-product-compliance
Lightning Source LLC
Chambersburg PA
CBHW020325160726
47992CB00004B/1707